Designing and Making Handwrought Jewelry

Joseph F. Shoenfelt

McGraw-Hill Book Company, Inc.
New York   Toronto   London

DESIGNING AND MAKING HANDWROUGHT JEWELRY

Library of Congress Catalog Card Number: 60–10613

First Edition

First published as a McGraw-Hill Paperback in 1963.

8910 MUMU 7654
ISBN 07-057004-3

ACKNOWLEDGMENTS

* * * * * * * * * * * * * * * * * * * *

I would like to acknowledge here some of those friends, craftsmen and students, who have made this book possible. In Mexico, Antonio Pineda, Antonio Castillo, Kent Bowman, the Beckmans, Simon Yebarra and Jim Pinto gave information, advice and examples of their work.

A few of the many students whose work furnished most of the illustrations in the book are: Ron and Tess Burk, Irving Griffee, Benson Murray, Jerry Schoenblum, Criss Rossbach, Robert Foultz, Ellen Alsdorf, John Masson, Ben Foster, Elmo Barden, Elizabeth O'Conner, Audrey Orloff, Nancy Nugent, Clarence Becker, Sam Swart, Donna Cooper, June Langer, Jim Schoonover, Bill Johnson, John Fitzpatrick, Tony Davi, Marvin Skinner, Jim McGuire, Lawrence Marrish, Tom Giannetti, Ronald Oshier, Claude Merrill, Lucille Millis, Shirley Stern, Rodger Goodman and Joan Kane.

My special thanks go to Richard Bohall, who helped with the photography, and my son, Joe Evan Shoenfelt, who assisted with lights, cameras and the many details involved in photographing jewelry.

A PLAN OF APPROACH

✳ ✳ ✳ ✳ ✳ ✳ ✳ ✳ ✳ ✳ ✳ ✳ ✳ ✳ ✳ ✳ ✳ ✳ ✳ ✳

This work is designed to provide much that is not available in any other publication on jewelry-making. It has some unique features, planned to meet those needs felt by the writer as both teacher and craftsman. For example, generalizations are not made until the specifics have been discussed and illustrated. Processes and techniques progress from the simple or easier ones to perform to the more difficult. For the more advanced reader it may be necessary to peruse only briefly the basic processes, but he may find something new even in these sections. The techniques are also arranged in the order in which they are used.

Cross referencing provides easy access to information or techniques as they are needed. The drawings and photographs are presented from the vantage point of the actual worker rather than from the often misleading viewpoint of the observer on the other side of the worktable.

While function, form, and technique are considered as a whole unit, function and form are presented after some experience has been gained with the processes and techniques; if they must be separated for discussion, their relative importance would tend to place first emphasis upon design aspects. This section is organized in a manner similar to that on techniques and processes.

In addition to the section on tools, materials, and sources of supply, a section is devoted to solving the type of problem often encountered by many craftsmen in jewelry. Too many good designs are spoiled and too many students are frustrated by simple problems that can be corrected with a little knowledge of this type. Perhaps more important, a great deal of time can be salvaged to produce more and better jewelry.

This book could not have been completed without the aid of my students, who have at one time or another committed all the errors in creating jewelry and have learned how to correct them. The *Solving Your Problems* section is a direct result of their endeavors. To them also I am indebted for many of the pieces of jewelry included in the photographs.

Without a sabbatical leave from the State University of New York I could not have found the energy or time to devote myself to the preparation of this work.

My special gratitude goes to my wife, Ann Shoenfelt, who has been a constant source of encouragement and an invaluable aid in compiling this book. I also want to thank my Canadian friend, Helen Magee, and Malina Faulkner, who aided in the preparation of the manuscript.

I must acknowledge my debt to all my fellow craftsmen, both in the United States and in Mexico, who through many conversations and demonstrations have contributed greatly to this experimental approach to jewelry, and have consented kindly to allow photographs of their work to be used.

The following quotations will help to establish a philosophy or frame of reference for our approach to jewelry:

"Ultimately all confusion of values proceeds from the same source:—neglect of the intrinsic significance of the medium, a special language having its own characteristics, is the source of every art. . . ." *

"The crafts, in short, provide opportunities to make works of art; they have actually been the school of feeling (feeling becomes clear and conscious only through its symbols), as they were the incentives to articulation and the first formulators of abstractive vision." **

"What we commonly understand as 'originality' often depends on the successful integration of the symbol as a visual entity with all other elements, pointed to a particular problem, performing a specific function consistent with its form. Its use at the proper time and place is essential and its misuse will inevitably result in banality or mere affectation. The designer's capacity to contribute to the effectiveness of the symbols' basic meaning by interpretation,

---

* From *Art as Experience* by John Dewey, copyright 1934 by John Dewey. Published by Minton, Balch & Co. Used by permission of G. P. Putnam's Sons, New York.

** By permission of Susanne K. Langer, *Feeling and Form,* Charles Scribner's Sons, New York, 1953.

addition, subtraction, juxtaposition, alteration, adjustment, association, intensification and clarification, is parallel to those qualities we call 'original.' " ***

*** By permission of Paul Rand, *Thoughts on Design,* Wittenborn and Company, New York, 1947.

CONTENTS

* *

1 ✳ AN INTRODUCTION TO JEWELRY

✳ ✳ ✳ ✳ ✳ ✳ ✳ ✳ ✳ ✳ ✳ ✳ ✳ ✳ ✳ ✳ ✳ ✳ ✳ ✳

Making jewelry can be fun. But, like painting, writing, or playing golf, it requires skill and ability—and luckily each of us has at least some skill in manipulating materials, which can be used in the craft of jewelry-making. Very few people shoot par golf, yet the challenge is there and we continue to strive toward that goal. During the past decade more and more people have turned to crafts, including jewelry-making, for a challenging and rewarding experience. Most have found satisfaction and pleasure. Professionals in their own fields who are amateur craftsmen for pleasure know that the richest satisfactions of jewelry-making do not come in easy lessons or with follow-the-steps copies.

This fact is the major reason for this book. I hope to bridge the gap between the purely technical and elementary approaches with some of the thinking processes fundamental to all arts and crafts and thus approach a higher creative level. Many books for beginners are aimed too far below the creative possibilities of the part-time craftsman or student; they are unsatisfactory to the amateur who wishes to move on

1

to a higher level. Certainly a person needs techniques, the best available, because they influence the design; but function, form, and technique provide the whole, and one without the others is like soup without salt. What a student makes and how he makes it must inevitably be his own creative decision. There are, however, many general ideas, which when mulled over and used along with the basic techniques, can stimulate an individual and personal approach. These solutions of function and form are as useful as the knowledge of how to solder two pieces of metal together.

The formation of jewelry and decorative objects was one of man's earliest achievements. The progress of the civilization of ancient Egypt is marked by examples of jewelry from the First Dynasty (about 5500 B.C.) to the time of Cleopatra and the Romans. This jewelry was emblematic and allegorical, taking the form of the scarab (sacred sun beetle), the utchat (sacred eye), the ureus (hooded snake), and the human-headed hawk. It was worn as diadems, earrings, pendants, necklaces, chains, frontlets, side disks, pectoral jewels, rings, bracelets (used both below and above the elbow), and other trinkets.

The Old Testament makes many references to jewelry; some of them indicate an advanced state of knowledge and technique in the art of working precious metals as well as setting the stones.

Every age and race of people has lavished much time and energy, art and craftsmanship on the production of jewelry. Greek jewelry possessed a refined delicacy. In early Roman times jewelry was simple and used in ceremonial rites. Later, as imperial luxury developed, cameos and elaborate jewelry of all kinds—including hairpins—were in great demand. Prehistoric jewelry from northern Europe indicates that a heavy architectural form was used to create fascinating fibulas, torques, and rude animal shapes. Much medieval jewelry was large, rectangular, heavily carved, and set with many stones. The great splendor of Renaissance jewelry reflects the times, and such jewelers as Benvenuto Cellini gloried in the extravagances of elaborate arabesques. In the France of Louis XIV the abusive use of precious stones began; jewelry became nothing but clusters of stones. It was jewelry devoid of any merit in design or craftsmanship. We are perhaps still in a period of transition from those abuses to a more refined art of jewelry-making.

Throughout the world peasant jewelry, with its directness and naïve charm, has often served as a basis for the jewelry of the upper classes and nobility. This was especially true if the ornament originated in a foreign land, which gave a mystic quality to the jewelry, but peasant jewelry itself shows little influence from such sources. Each culture has tended to produce its own symbolic devices which were the most expressive and revered by the group.

Knowledge of ancient jewelry comes from three major sources: first, representation in carvings or on pottery; second, rare specimens of genuine pieces; third, funeral jewelry discovered in tombs throughout the world. In Mexico I had the pleasure of visiting many pyramids, including Monte Alban where Tomb 7 was discovered a few years ago. In this single tomb Mixtec jewelry valued at millions of dollars was recovered and placed in the Museum at Oaxaca where it can now be admired. There have also been great discoveries of jewelry in Egypt. We do not need to travel to the corners of the earth to see and be inspired by these ancient craftsmen, however. There are many fine examples of jewelry from various countries and ages in our own museums. You will find listed in the bibliography several books covering these fascinating products of the past which also provide valuable insights concerning people who preceded us on this earth.

The function of jewelry from the beginning of man's habitation on earth has been to give pleasure to the wearer, to enhance his appearance, to attract attention, and to fulfill the human need for self-aggrandizement. This function has not changed throughout the ages; only the style of jewelry has changed.

The making of decorative devices and symbols is one of man's oldest crafts; it started before man could make his own clothes and it remains today in our American economic system one of the few skilled occupations. This fascinating craft is being adopted by part-time hobbyists, educators, and therapists for its appeal and for its educational and therapeutic value. Unfortunately, until comparatively recent years, many techniques and methods of working have been the exclusive possession of the jewelry craftsman, who disclosed them only to his apprentices.

It is the purpose of this book, then, to make available to both beginners and advanced craftsmen the most simple and practical techniques of handwrought jewelry-making. Some are new and make use of modern technical advancements; others are old, tried-and-true methods, but in each case only the necessary ones have been included. They have been used over many years and gathered from many craftsmen in the United States, Sweden, Denmark, and Mexico. This book is addressed, therefore, to the amateur craftsman, the art and industrial art teacher, the therapist, and the hard-working student.

2 ✳ GETTING STARTED

✳ ✳

WIRE—BASIC PROCESS 1

Some fine jewelry can be made using only wire, without any soldering. This is a good beginning, since you can make a few simple pieces of jewelry that are completely your own from start to finish. Few tools are needed, and wire is readily available. This process alone could provide an amateur a lifetime of experimentation without exhausting all the inherent possibilities. Students of mine have worked in this manner from age 8 to 80, and all have been successful at their own level.

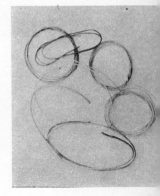

✳ *Materials*

    Wire: copper, brass, and sterling silver. I prefer silver, which can be obtained in many forms, but to start let us experiment with round wire in gauges from No. 10 to No. 16. Most wire comes in Brown and Sharpe (B&S) gauge—the smaller the number, the larger the wire.

7

Table 1

Thickness (inches)	B&S gauge	Uses
.128	8	A little large to start with
.102	10	Pins, necklaces, bracelets
.081	12	Pins, necklaces, earrings, bracelets
.064	14	Earrings, pins
.051	16	Earrings
.040	18	Too small for beginning, these will be useful in many ways later.
.032	20	
.025	22	

Sterling wire may also be obtained in:
square■ ,
triangular▲ ,
and half round ◖ .

Solid copper electric cable with the insulation removed can be used (the braided variety is too small), and copper and brass wire can be obtained from most supply houses and hardware stores. Brass wire works well and has a pleasant, warm color. Its one disadvantage is that it is slightly harder to work than silver or copper and must be annealed more often.

✳ *Tools* Fingers can do much of the job but we can find ways of supplementing our own strength and dexterity.

Pliers of all kinds may be used. (Unintentional marks on the metal are undesirable and should be filed off later, so we can use tape [Scotch, masking, or friction] over the jaws of serrated pliers.) Most jewelry pliers have smooth jaws made of relatively soft tool steel to reduce unwanted marks. The three most useful pliers are:
the chain-nose pliers with ◒ jaws,

the half-round or optician's pliers with ⬤ jaws, and the round-nose with ⦂ jaws;
other pliers will also prove useful. A pair of diagonal cutting pliers is the only tool needed to cut the wire to the desired length.

✳ *Tool and supply check list*
    Wire: copper, brass, or sterling silver
    Pliers: 1 diagonal cutting pliers
            1 chain-nose pliers
            1 half-round nose pliers
            1 round-nose pliers
    File: (to increase the variety of textures) No. 2
        smooth cut; Swiss pattern half-round 6″ long
    Hammer: 8-ounce ball peen
    Anvil or stake
    Abrasive: steel wool, emery, or crocus cloth

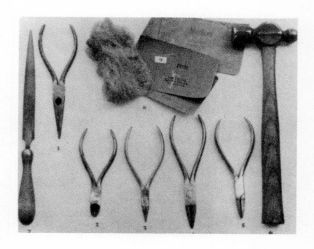

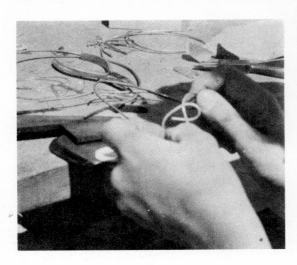

Use curves before introducing angles and straight lines. Graceful curves are formed easily with fingers alone.

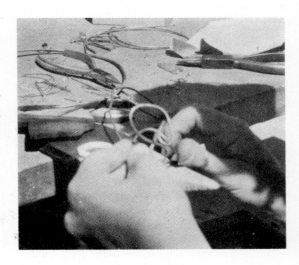

Solder: Soft or lead (50-50) (½ & ½) half and
half are common names. [Used for experiments
only]
Consult Appendix B for the sources of tools and
materials.

SOME EXPERIMENTS

Let's start with some *14-gauge round wire;* begin
by bending it with your fingers. How does it react to
pressure? Does it bend easily? What kind of bends
can be made with fingers alone?

Now you want a sharper bend that cannot be made
with the fingers, so try some pliers. Are there curves?
How about a straight line? Does it make the curves
look better, or is it too much of a contrast? Maybe
a slight curve should be added, perhaps another
straight line. Is it too long or too short? Variety adds
interest; repetition creates rhythm. You must decide
for yourself: It is good, excellent, or poor, solely on
the basis of your own judgment.

At this stage it might help to lay the wire on a
sheet of paper. Look at it. What about the shadows?
With a pencil you can add new lines or change the
present ones. Draw other combinations—now the
wire, now the pencil. Compare and select what fits
best. Check the scale. Is it too large or too small?
Make the wire do what you want it to do, back and
forth until there is a pleasing relationship of line and
space. Remember that the space between the wires
is just as important as the line created by the wire.
If it doesn't suit you, put it aside and try another
piece of wire, but save the first piece. Put it in your
scrap box. Perhaps the new one will suggest a solu-

Select the type of plier that matches the curve or direction you want to bend the wire—chain-nose for straight lines and sharp bends, half-round for smooth, flowing lines, round-nose for small curves and spirals.

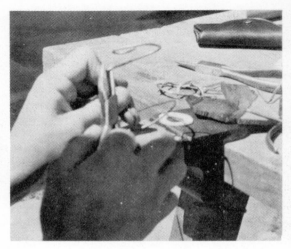

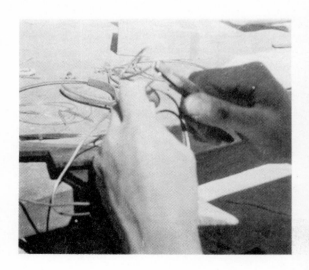

tion for the first design. Thicker wire might work better. Can you make a pin of it? Or would it work as a pendant, if it were larger? Duplicated on a smaller scale, with thinner wire, it might make nice earrings.

Here are a few suggestions from my own sketchbooks and scrap box to compare with yours. One idea will lead to another; the important thing is to keep experimenting.

Experiment with various lengths of wire to help add variety to the line and space. All designs in these illustrations were made with less than one foot of wire.

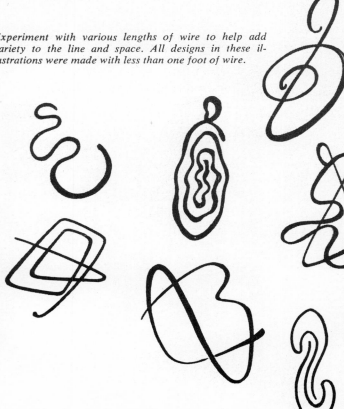

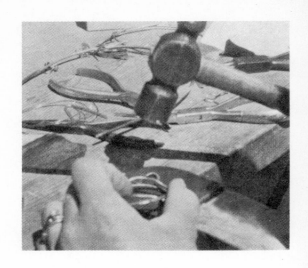

Move the wire apart to make it possible to pound the wire where you want it to be flat. Hit the wire smartly. Don't be afraid of spoiling it, but try to keep the face of the hammer flat to avoid nicking the wire. It is easy to blend a flat area into a curved one by using less pressure as you hit the wire.

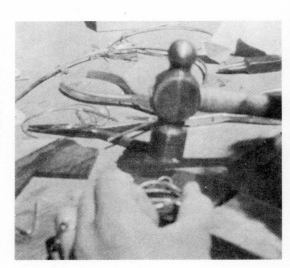

Now for some refinements. Is there enough variety
in the work? Is there nice repetition of lines and
spaces? Would a wider line be better? If so, pound
the wire with a hammer on a hardwood or metal
surface. Notice what happens to the wire. If it gets
too hard to work it should be annealed (Chapter 4).
Sometimes it is wise to anneal the wire before starting to work. To make the wire smaller, file part of
it away. A flattened piece of wire turned sideways
will also be thin; you can thus have thick or thin
depending upon the angle of view.

What textures can be made with the hammer?
With the file? Now and then it is a good idea to shine
the wire with some steel wool to get a better idea of
what you have accomplished.

On the next page are a few more tricks of the trade
to add more variety to the your collection of samples.
Keep your scraps and experiments in a box. (I call it
an idea box; many good projects are suggested by
looking it over from time to time.)

TURNING YOUR EXPERIMENTS INTO JEWELRY

By now you should have some feel of the metal
and know more about the limitation and potential
of wire. If you haven't already solved the problem
of turning your experiments into wearable jewelry,
here are some possibilities:

Pendants require some means of fastening the jewelry to the neck chain. A simple loop of wire will
work; it can repeat the general character of the wire
design. For the neckpiece, leather thongs, nylon shoe-
laces, round velvet ribbons, wire, and of course chains
can be used.

Make small curves and wiggles by wrapping the wire halfway around the round-nose pliers. The size is controlled by the location of the wire on the pliers.

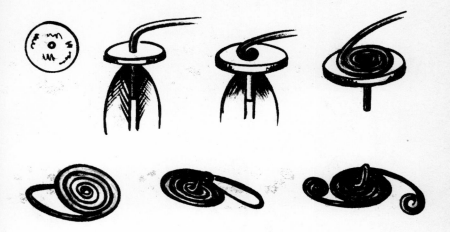

Spirals are made easily by using a disc about the size
of a penny with a hole drilled in its center. Place the
wire through the hole and hold it from the back with
a ring clamp, wrench, or pliers. Pull the wire snug and
coil the wire around itself. Repeat the process on each
end of the wire to make a double spiral.

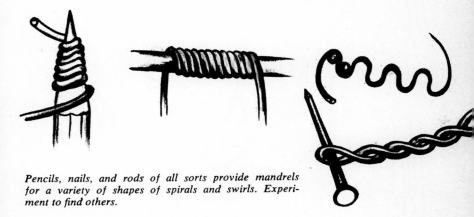

Pencils, nails, and rods of all sorts provide mandrels
for a variety of shapes of spirals and swirls. Experiment to find others.

Make the loop at ninety degrees to permit the pendant to hang with its best side front. If the end of the wire is pounded and filed, it will look more finished.

More pendants.

Earrings. Findings can be obtained from most supply houses in copper, silver, and gold finishes. At the moment you need a dangle-type ear finding, which has a loop to attach the wire dangles you have made. It may require some filing to make them fit and hang freely. Remember that earrings should be made for the right and left ears and are exact duplicates only some of the time. The same forms can be used for earrings and pendants, but there is a difference of scale.

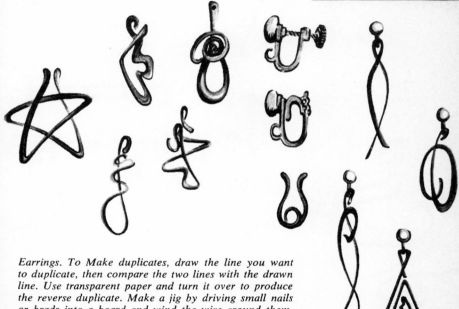

Earrings. To Make duplicates, draw the line you want to duplicate, then compare the two lines with the drawn line. Use transparent paper and turn it over to produce the reverse duplicate. Make a jig by driving small nails or brads into a board and wind the wire around them. You may need more than one jig to produce the shapes you desire for one design.

Pins can be made (for this problem they should be made a part of the design) from the ends of the wire. One end becomes the catch. The other, which becomes the pin, should be filed to a point so that it will not damage the clothing on which it is worn. Balance must be considered. The pin should be above the center so that the jewelry will hang well.

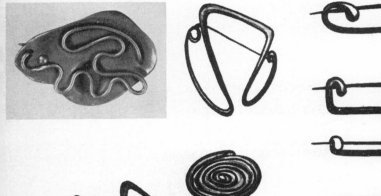

Pins and brooches. Make a hook in one end of the wire (before you start) to serve as a catch. It may be cut off later if you don't need it. Save two or three inches of wire at the other end of the wire for the pin tang. To harden the tang and make it easier to hold for filing, pound its entire length. File the pin small enough to avoid its making holes in closely woven fabrics. There are so many possibilities here that it is impossible to estimate the amount of wire needed, but eighteen inches is an adequate length to start with.

Some alphabet pins. The alphabet provides ideas for pins and pendants. These illustrated were made with 15 inches of 12- or 14-gauge wire. The C has been pounded to give better variety to the line. The pin tang (dotted lines) should be filed to reduce its size. One end of the wire makes the tang; the other provides the catch.

Other kinds of jewelry:

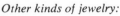

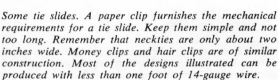

Some tie slides. A paper clip furnishes the mechanical requirements for a tie slide. Keep them simple and not too long. Remember that neckties are only about two inches wide. Money clips and hair clips are of similar construction. Most of the designs illustrated can be produced with less than one foot of 14-gauge wire.

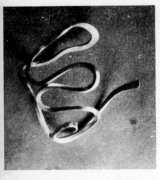

Bracelets. *Heavier wire is needed for most arm decorations. Use 10- or 12-gauge wire for the illustrated designs; it provides ample strength and spring. Bend the bracelet around a piece of pipe or a can if a bracelet mandrel is not available. A leather mallet will not mark the wire, but will aid in shaping the bracelet. If both sides of the bracelet are the same, you need only to design one side and then reverse it, to save time.*

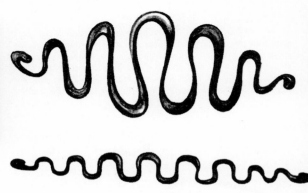

PROCESSES NEEDED FOR WIRE JEWELRY

* *Shaping: bending* Much of the work with wire can be done by hand if the metal is soft, but for smaller bands and pieces of jewelry, pliers, hammers, mallets, and stakes are used. After a little experimentation with various kinds of pliers you will soon discover many ways of creating any desired shape. Some bends can be more easily made with the pliers held in front of the curve, others will be easier if the wire is held with one pair of pliers and bent with another. A square bend is simple if the pliers are clamped tight at each side of the angle. The clamping action of the pliers will straighten the wire up to the angle of the band.

* *Shaping: hammering* Some bends are made before hammering (in fact, cannot be made after the wire is flat) and others are made after the wire is flat—it depends on the direction of the bend and the effect desired. Experiment to see which will work more easily. Take care not to pound the wires that overlap; they tend to cut each other. Keep the wire soft and don't pound too much after it gets hard. It is better to take time to anneal the metal—it will save time. An anvil, stake, or any steel plate will provide a working surface to pound on. To save the hammer, don't pound the steel—only the wire. Any hammer will work, but keep the head smooth and clean with emery cloth and steel wool. Later you may want to obtain some special hammers.

* *Annealing* (see Chapter 4 for a more detailed description) Silver, copper, and brass (hammered, cut, bent, twisted, or drawn) become hard and brittle when worked and should be annealed (softened). Heat the metal over an open flame (Bunsen burner, kitchen gas range) or with a torch until it is a dull red and about 1000° Fahrenheit. When the metal has lost this red color, it may be dropped into pickle or water to cool. The metal should be annealed as frequently as is necessary in order to maintain its malleability.

✳ *Filing* If a line (wire) appears too large, you can reduce its size by filing. This is as simple as filing your nails. For our purpose a No. 2 smooth-cut Swiss pattern, half-round 6″ file will serve adequately. A file cuts in the forward direction. Therefore, exert pressure on the forward stroke and release pressure on the return (see page 26). For filing inside surfaces and corners use the round side of the file. The file should move in the direction of the surface rather than across it. Always work away from the finished surface to avoid scratches on the finished work. Holding the piece to be filed is often more difficult than the actual filing. To make it easier, use a bench pin as illustrated to provide a rest for the jewelry. Don't be afraid to file the wood; this helps you guide the file and makes the whole operation much easier. The file is not intended as a shaping tool, but it will refine or true edges and surfaces. It is also used for smoothing aberrations and removing scratches and tool marks. It is an operation preliminary to using emery paper and steel wool. Several of the better jewelers I know think that the filing gives any piece of jewelry its true character.

✳ *Drawing wire* If smaller-gauge wire is desired and you do not have it readily available, a large wire can be made smaller by using a draw-plate. To accomplish this, file one end of annealed wire to a point that will go through the holes in the draw-plate and stick out about ½" on the other side. Place the wire in a hole just slightly smaller than the wire and grasp the filed end with a pair of pliers or draw-tongs. Pull the wire completely through the plate. Repeat, using the next smaller hole, until you have the gauge you want. If the wire becomes too stiff, anneal it before continuing. Usually this is necessary every three or four holes. Wax or oil will lubricate the wire as it is drawn.

✳ *Cleaning the metal* (see Chapter 3 for a detailed description of pickling.) When metals containing copper are heated, an oxide, which should be removed, forms on the surface. This can be done with steel wool or emery cloth but it is easier to use chemicals.

✳ *Finishing* (see Chapter 3)

JEWELRY FINDINGS AND THEIR APPLICATION

Ear wires, pinbacks, necklace catches, cufflink backs, and the other working parts on jewelry are called *findings*. Commercial findings for jewelry are so well made and inexpensive that I advise their use for all jewelry except where the finding is an integral part of the design. This is especially true for the beginner with limited time at his disposal. The time required to make such things as catches can be better

Good filing position using a V block or bench pin to help support the jewelry as you work.

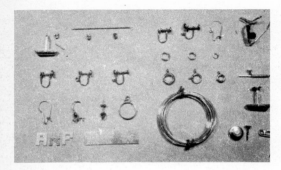

Some of the many ready-made jewelry findings available.

spent on design practice. Most findings are applied after the jewelry is finished, but provision should be made for and consideration given to the type and placement of the working mechanisms. In all cases the finding should be placed above the center of balance; otherwise a brooch, for example, will not hang properly and will have a tendency to flip over.

In the accompanying illustrations you will see the most useful findings. They are all easily available at your supply house, and some of them may be bought in variety stores or hobby shops. For more varied and less common findings consult your supplier's catalogue.

3 ∗ THE FINISHING TECHNIQUES: FINISHING, POLISHING, BUFFING, OXIDIZING

∗ ∗

Now that you have made a few pieces of jewelry, it is time to learn how to finish them. For our purpose, finishing will include all of the final processes that may be used to create the desired effect on the metal surface. The surface of nonferrous metals—copper, brass, silver and gold—if properly prepared, may be polished to a soft luster (satin or butler's finish) or a high mirror finish. Almost any stage of the finishing process may produce the final finish. *Polishing* is done by hand or by motor buff and may be as important a part of the total effect as the shape. It should therefore be studied from the standpoint of how it will best enhance the piece of jewelry.

TOOLS AND MATERIALS

For Hand Polishing and Buffing
(the ones marked ∗ are needed to start)

∗Steel wool	Fine, #00 or #000	Hardware or department store
∗Emery cloth	Fine, #0 to #000	
Crocus cloth	Very fine	

*Felt hand buff	You can make these very easily	
Chamois hand buff	(See sketch)	
Tripoli	For polishing	Obtained from all supply houses
Jeweler's rouge	For buffing	

Soft cloth, soap, kitchen cleanser, small brush (toothbrush works well)

To Remove Scratches before Polishing

*Smooth-cut 6″ file	#2 or 3 cut	Can be obtained from
Needle files	#2 cut	most supply houses.
Riffle files	#2 cut	See Appendix B.
*Burnisher		Many of these items
Scotch stone		may also be bought at
Pumice or kitchen cleanser		local hardware and drug stores.

For Motor Polishing and Buffing (additional)

Buffing motor. Any ¼-h.p. or larger electric motor will work by adding tapered spindles; regular polishing machines can be obtained inexpensively from most supply houses. I often use an electric hand drill mounted in its bracket as a polishing motor, and a great variety of wheels are now available at most hardware stores.
Muslin polishing wheel for rouge   4″ or 5″
Flannel buffing wheel for tripoli   4″ or 5″
Lea Compound may be used instead of tripoli and works better for motor polishing.

For Oxidizing

Glass jar, Pyrex dish, or enameled pan with lid
Potassium sulfide (commonly called Liver of Sulfur)
Wooden or copper tongs
Small brush
These are the basic requirements. Add others as they are needed.

Hand polishing and buffing sticks may be made
simply by gluing strips of felt or chamois to sticks.
Each stick should be about one foot long. Emery
sticks may be made in the same way and are very
useful for removing scratches. Use them as you would
a file; like the buff sticks, they may be obtained from
supply houses if you desire.

HAND POLISHING AND BUFFING

* *Preparing the metal* Before it is polished, the metal
should be clean and as free from scratches and rough
spots as possible. Prepare wire pieces for polishing
by rubbing them with emery paper and steel wool.
(This may be all the finish required.) The preparation of sheet metal is often a more involved process,
especially if the metal has been scraped or filed to
remove scratches or solder.

Basically, the principle involved in finishing any
surface is to proceed from a coarse abrasive through
medium to fine abrasives. The procedure is: *first,*
file (coarse to smooth- or fine-cut) in only one direction if possible [*This applies to all abrasives*]; *second,*
remove the file marks with emery cloth; *third,* use
steel wool for a satin matte finish to complete the
process. If at any stage you find scratches, go back
rather than continue with the finer abrasive—it really
saves time.

* *Polishing and buffing* A high mirror finish may be
obtained by using finer and finer abrasives. This includes polishing, which is still an abrasive action in
which metal is cut away. Polishing is followed by
buffing, a combination cutting and burnishing action.

Actually, molecules of the metal are pushed around (but not removed) to provide a very smooth bright surface. To accomplish this, use a hand polishing stick charged with tripoli. To charge the stick, rub the felt over a piece of tripoli, and it will pick up enough tripoli to produce the necessary abrasive action when rubbed on the metal with a backward-and-forward motion. Buffing is done in the same manner, except that jeweler's rouge is used and a chamois buff stick is more efficient. *Do not* mix the compounds on the same buffing stick. To get into difficult or inside places, thread a string rubbed with jeweler's rouge through loops or holes in the jewelry. A very high mirror finish can also be obtained by rubbing the metal with a smooth steel rod or a burnisher. Dip the burnisher in water, as shown, for best results.

✳ *Machine or motor polishing and buffing* It is obvious that a polishing or buffing wheel turning at 1700 rpm or more will cut or burnish the metal surface much faster than the hand process. There are, however, many situations where a machine will not work, such as finishing chains or pieces with sharp points. Motor polishing and buffing supplement the hand process but do not replace it.

When polishing or buffing with a motor buff, follow the same principles as in finishing by hand. The difference between hand and motor buffing lies in the variety of shapes and kinds of wheel available for the motor (consult your supply catalogue). There are soft muslin and flannel buffs made in layers; hard felt buffs, some shaped to polish the inside of rings; brass- and steel-wire and bristle brushes for scratch finishes; and many other types for a great variety of

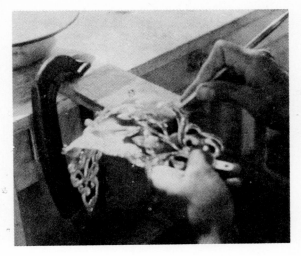

Photos show a section of a
crown being burnished by a
Mexican silversmith who
added a small piece of sea
weed to the water. A touch
of soap produces the same
effect.

Correct polishing position.

purposes. It is not necessary to have more than one muslin and one flannel buff for most jobs, although a hard felt buff is often useful. The motor buffer is simply an electric motor of ⅛ or ¼ horsepower equipped with tapered spindles on each end of the main shaft. An adapter for small thin wheels and the spindles can be obtained from most supply houses; with these any motor may be converted to a buffing motor. The buffs are screwed onto the spindle by hand. The spindle revolves toward the operator. The left-hand spindle has a left-hand thread, therefore the buff for that side should be screwed onto the spindle with a counterclockwise direction. This arrangement prevents the buffs from unscrewing when the motor is running. An electric hand drill will work well as a buffing machine when mounted in a bench mount.

Remember that tripoli is an abrasive, while rouge is a polish; to mix the two on one wheel will ruin it for both. Experience has shown that tripoli should be used on muslin or hard felt buffs and rouge on the others. To use the motor buff, charge the wheel with tripoli by holding a tripoli stick against the wheel for a few moments while it is revolving. Do the same thing with rouge. The jewelry to be polished or buffed is then held in the fingers and pressed firmly against the wheel below the center or spindle, as illustrated. By moving the metal around, all parts of the piece will be brought into contact with the wheel. Do not polish or buff only one spot at a time, as uneven results will be obtained. Usually five or ten minutes is required for the preliminary polish. If the jewelry surface is irregular, recessed, or made of wire, take care not to catch the piece in the revolving wheel.

A soft flexible wheel such as muslin is best for such pieces as well as for polishing inside areas.

Wash the piece after it is polished to remove the tripoli before proceeding to buffing with rouge. This can be done simply by washing in soap and water with a soft brush such as a toothbrush. As suggested before, use a flannel buff charged with jeweler's rouge for the final polish. This operation produces a high mirror finish. As a final step, wash the piece again to remove any grease and finger marks and dry with a clean cloth.

There are several very fine polishing cloths on the market which are useful for putting a final polish on the piece of jewelry. They also remove fingerprints and help prevent discoloration.

CHEMICAL FINISHES

✷ *Oxidized or antique finish*　As the finished piece of jewelry ages, it will eventually become black. Nature will do this because various elements cause the metal to darken and color. This process, known as oxidizing, may be controlled, however, and is used by craftsmen to color the metal, to bring out the modeling or form and otherwise enhance the beauty of the metal. Most metals commonly used for jewelry may be oxidized by the use of a sulfur compound, although some metals require other chemicals.

To oxidize silver or copper, dissolve in a cup of water a lump of liver of sulfur (potassium sulfide) about ½" in diameter. As the liver of sulfur grows older it will lose its strength and a larger lump will be needed. The dissolving may be hastened by heating in a Pyrex or enameled container. After the metal

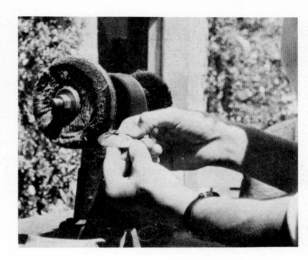

Correct buffing position.

is polished and clean, drop it into this solution—which can be used hot or cold. (If the metal is not thoroughly clean, it will not oxidize evenly.) The solution may be brushed on if only a portion of the metal is to be made black—successive brushings with a small camel's-hair brush will produce the desired color. Steel wool dipped into the solution and rubbed on the metal will also oxidize the metal. When the metal has reached the desired color, remove, wash, and dry it. Generally the solution will work better hot, or the metal may be heated and dropped into the cold solution with similar results. If the solution is too strong or the metal is left too long in the solution, the coating may become too thick. In such cases it is wise to remove the oxide and start over again.

This process is completed by removing the unwanted blackened or oxidized surface with fine steel wool, pumice powder, kitchen cleanser, or rouge, either by hand or machine. This finish may be buffed if care is taken that not too much of the finish is removed. Iodine is sometimes used on silver; it produces a blue or black color on gold.

✷ *Bright dip* A bright dip may be made by mixing equal parts of sulphuric and nitric acid, adding the sulphuric to the nitric acid. A pinch of table salt makes the solution better. Remember that this is acid—it is very corrosive and must be used carefully, but it will produce a bright surface on copper and brass. It is also used to remove fire scale or oxides (the dark gray spots) which often appear on silver when it is heated. Often these spots are not noticed until the metal is polished. They may be removed by continued polishing or by dipping into a bright-dip solution. Since the bright dip is concentrated acid and works very fast, take care. Do not leave the metal in the solution more than a few seconds. This also produces a soft matte finish on silver.

* *Preserving the finish* There is no perfect way to preserve some finishes, but it is only natural to try. Techniques used by craftsmen and dealers may help you. Some use lacquers on brass and copper (this also prevents the skin discoloration that some people suffer). To apply lacquer to the metal, it must be thin (cut with lacquer thinner). The clean jewelry can then be dipped in the lacquer or the lacquer may be brushed or sprayed on; the handy spray cans are best. You can obtain these from most art and jewelry supply houses. Plastic sprays such as Krylon can also be used, but remember the metal is covered as with lacquer and it loses its true metal quality. Wax— such as beeswax, floor wax, and car wax—may be applied and polished with a piece of soft cloth or flannel. This may be repeated occasionally with very little effort. Buffing also leaves a thin coating of wax on the metal which will help preserve the finish.

To remove fingermarks from a highly polished surface, many jewelry stores use a little ammonia in water and then wipe dry with a soft cloth or tissue paper. There are also on the market various cleaning solutions and cloths which may be used. Most of these will remove tarnish and may be used as a final polish. I have found that my students like the results the cloths produce so well that my classes wear out one or two polish cloths each semester.

The matte or butler's finish on silver probably requires less care for its preservation, another reason it is so popular with most craftsmen and people who know fine silver.

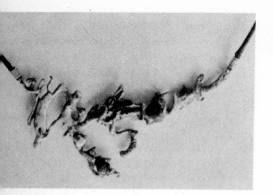

Fused silver and brass necklace, made by a young abstract painter, and a fused silver pendant with polished citrine stone.

4 * ANNEALING, SOLDERING, PICKLING, AND FUSING METALS

* *

THE PROCESSES REQUIRING HEAT

Soldering cannot be avoided in making most jewelry, and by now you probably have some ideas for pieces that require joints. Hard or silver solder, requiring high temperatures to melt, is the material used on most metals to create strong and durable joints the color of silver. This type of solder, used in many industrial processes for its strength and resistance to vibration, has also been used by craftsmen for several centuries. A less strong joint may be produced by soft lead solder (low melting point) which is often used to attach such jewelry findings as pinbacks. This is the kind of solder used by your plumber and TV repairman. These will be discussed separately to avoid confusion. Annealing was mentioned briefly in Chapter 1 but will be discussed more fully here. A third process, fusing, which requires heat, will be discussed later in this chapter. Pickling will be discussed in this chapter because it is used with all the heat processes.

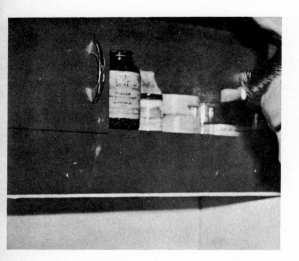

A convenient soldering arrangement using city gas and a foot bellows to provide the air. For individual shops it is desirable to have the heating equipment at the worktable or bench.

Tools and materials (I recommend the ones marked
   * as a start.)
Heat sources for soldering (only *one* is necessary)
1. *Mouth or blow pipe—a basic tool if gas is available. Can be attached to kitchen range.
2. Acetylene tank and torch—a very good source for heat up to 2800°. Many craftsmen consider it to be the best, but it is expensive for the individual just starting. The total cost for a complete "Prest-O-lite" outfit is about $45.
3. *Propane or Bernz-o-matic Torch—a good starting outfit for home use with advantages similar to the one above. Can be purchased in most hardware stores for $5 to $8; the disposable cans (which cost about $1.50) burn for six hours.

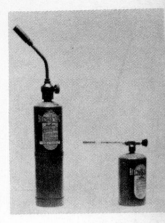

4. Air–gas soldering torch—a good source of heat with foot bellows, air compressor, or some other source of compressed air when gas is available.
5. Gasoline blowtorch—satisfactory for large work or experienced craftsmen, but very tricky for the inexperienced. (Nearly all soldering in Taxco is done with this source of heat.)
6. Jet King—pocket-size butane blowtorch provides intense (3500°) pinpoint flame for 30 minutes on each charger. Torch and one charger cost about $2. Torch jet charges (box of two) cost about 40¢.
7. *Soldering iron—for soft soldering only. A small electric soldering pencil is satisfactory, or the gun-type instant-heating iron may be used.

Solders
1. Silver solder—*Easy Flow, which melts at 1285° F. and flows at about 1325° is all that is required now. Other solders and their properties are indicated at the end of this section.
2. Lead solder—common names, 50–50, half-and-half, or soft solder may be obtained at any hardware store.

Fluxes (one is enough)
Borax cone, powder, or solution—the basic flux for centuries. "Twenty Mule Team" household borax will work nicely mixed to a paste with water.

Commercial fluxes
1. *Handy Flux—a prepared flux made by Handy & Harman is a good general-purpose flux.

2. Potassium fluoride—sometimes poisonous and not much better than borax.

3. T.B.H. Liquid Flouron flux—simple to use, preserves temper and color of metal.

4. Soldering paste or flux for soft soldering—the type used by the mechanic or TV repairman is cheap and easily available.

General supplies
*Charcoal block or asbestos pad
Scraper
Small camel's-hair brush
*Tweezers
*Soldering poker—piece of wire with a point filed on it. (Wire coat hangers work well.)
Binding wire—soft black iron wire in gauges ranging from 16 to 24
Clamps—can be made from coat-hanger wire, binding wire, cotter pins and paper clips
Spring-type clothespins

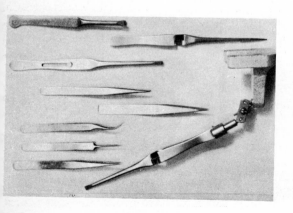

A few of the many tweezers available, including two with holding or clamping devices used for soldering and jewelry work.

Soldering clamps and tweezers are available and are very convenient.

Supplies for pickling

Glass jar, Pyrex dish, or earthenware crock. (An old
    battery case works well.)
*Sparex No. 2
Sulphuric acid
Copper or wood tongs

EXPERIMENTS

To increase your understanding of how metals react to heat and to learn how your designs for jewelry will be influenced by the technique involved, try these experiments:

Shot-making: Probably the best and simplest experiment is to take a small scrap of silver wire and learn to melt the silver. (Sheet silver may also be used.) Clean the silver with steel wool and place on an asbestos or charcoal block. Start with a small piece, ½ " more or less of 14- or 16-gauge wire. Put a little flux on the silver to exclude the oxides, or you can dip the silver in the flux with tweezers. You are now ready to apply the heat.

Let's notice at this point some of the characteristics of the torch flame. If you recall the Bunsen burner used in the chemistry lab, you will remember that the hottest part of the flame is at the tip of the blue or inner cone. You may also remember that by adjustment of the amount of air a cleaner or bluer flame resulted. For our purpose we want a clean blue flame with sufficient air to produce complete combustion of the gas. This will not only keep the metal cleaner but will also produce a hotter flame. We can vary the size of the flame by adjusting the amount of gas used. Less air will produce a softer flame, and more air will produce a sharper, more concentrated flame. Each heat source will have its own characteristics; you will learn them as you try this experiment. This is also a good way to check your heat when you change heat sources.

Now to get back to shot-making. The scraps of fluxed silver are on a fireproof surface. As the heat is applied, notice that the flux boils and bubbles. This occurs at about 212° Fahrenheit, the temperature at which water boils. That is exactly what is happening: the water in the flux is boiling away. The next important heat sign appears at about 900° F. You will notice a slight pink or reddish color in the metal. As the metal absorbs heat from the torch, the metal will continue to change color, becoming redder. At about 1200° the metal will appear a dull red. This is important as an indicator that the metal is annealed. You will notice that the flux has again become liquid. It will remain liquid, providing the protection for which it is used. Continue to apply the heat and the metal will change to a bright red (1400° to 1500°). Normally, for soldering, the silver should not be heated above this point. Now, however, we will continue to apply heat to the metal, observing the changes in the structure of the silver. You will notice that the surface of the metal begins to shimmer and actually to move slightly. At above 1640° the metal becomes a liquid. Keep the heat on it and the metal, as a result of surface tension, will roll itself into a ball or shot. It's as simple as that. Apply the heat, the silver will do the rest. Drop the shot into the pickle solution to clean it. If you want a round shot, make a round indentation in the asbestos or charcoal block; otherwise, the bottom of the shot will be flat.

These shots may be used in many ways in the construction and decoration of jewelry. For example, the shot may be soldered to the end of a piece of wire and used as interest centers, or they can be used to provide repetition or contrast by varying the size, or in combination with drilled holes.

To really test your heat source try this same experiment with copper. In some respects this metal provides a better test than silver, because you need about 2000 degrees of heat to melt copper.

Another interesting experiment to help gain better control of the heat and to understand the working characteristics of the metal is that of melting a drop or ball on the end of a wire. Place a piece of wire in an upright position or hold it with a pair of tongs or tweezers. Be sure to put flux on the end you wish to melt. Apply heat to the end of the wire until it melts and forms a ball. This requires more skill in using the torch: too much heat will melt the metal without forming a ball.

ANNEALING

Annealing is the heating process that removes the tensions, stresses, and hardness which form when craft metals are worked. Scientifically speaking, base metals—silver, copper, gold, and their alloys—become soft at certain temperatures, while ferrous metals —iron and steel—become hard because the grain or

Some Important Facts on Metal Properties
A code to help you recognize metal temperatures

Heat colors	Temperature	Useful information
Pink or first red	900° F.	
	1000°	
Dull red	1100°	Handy flux melts
	1200°	Good annealing temperatures
	1325°	Easy-flow solder melts or flows
Bright red	1400°	Do not heat silver
	1500°	above this point
Cherry red	1640°	Sterling silver melts
	1761°	Fine silver and commercial brass melt
	1980°	Copper melts

Solder	Content		Melting point
Soft solder	60% lead, 40% tin		400° F.
	50% lead, 50% tin		450°
Hard or silver solder			
*Easy Flow [1]	#40 [2]	65% silver	1325°
*Medium Flow	#30	70% silver	about 1390°
Hard	#20	72% silver	1425°
It	#10	80% silver	1460°

1. Handy & Harman, names
2. Hagstoz and Sons, numbers
          Other companies use similar solder
          designations

NOTE. There are some commercial silver or hard solders compounded to melt at about 1000° F., but their color does not match sterling, so their usefulness in the production of jewelry is limited.

* Most useful for hand craftsmen

molecular structure of the metal changes. For our purpose we simply heat the metal, silver, brass, or copper to a dull red and cool. To accomplish this, any adequate heat source is applied to the metal, care being taken to apply the heat evenly and all over the article. Do not concentrate the heat; it is better to use a soft blue flame. When the metal has reached dull red (1000° to 1200° F.), remove the heat. When the metal has lost the red color, it may be dropped in pickle (see page 52) or water to cool. Always be sure there is NO *soft solder* on the metal as it will burn into the metal and cause pits and scars. If there are small pieces, such as wire, be very careful not to melt them. A little experience will show you how much heat is required. This also provides you the knowledge necessary for the next operation—soldering—since you will know how color indicates the temperature, and you will thus be able to control the heat without burning the metal.

The steps in annealing are:

1. Place the metal on a charcoal or asbestos surface.
2. Heat to a dull red—1200° F. is enough.
3. Drop in water or pickle after metal loses red color.

SOLDERING WITH HARD OR SILVER SOLDER

Basically, hard or silver soldering is a method of joining metals by means of a silver alloy which fuses or melts at a lower temperature than the metals to be joined do. (See chart, page 48.) Several conditions must be met for successful uniting of metals. *First,* the metal must be *clean. Second,* there must be a *fit*—the two pieces to be joined must touch and be held in contact with each other: you cannot solder air. *Third,* oxides must be excluded from the areas to be joined and both solder and metal must be kept clean. *Fourth,* the correct solder and amount of heat must be applied to the metal.

Cleaning the metal   The areas to be soldered should be cleaned physically—scraped or sanded to ensure cleanliness and an unoxidized metal surface. Any grease, wax, or dirt will prevent the solder from flowing; even the oil from the fingers will cause trouble. So, keep it clean!

Making a fit   Be sure the two pieces (wire to wire, wire to sheet, sheet to sheet) actually make contact and are held in contact while heat is applied. This often requires more work than the actual soldering operation; it must be done carefully to ensure a well-soldered joint. Sometimes the metal itself will provide enough pressure to ensure good contact. If not, some other method of holding the pieces together must be devised. Black iron binding wire of all gauges can be used as a holder and is less likely to solder to the parts. Clamps or clips made from iron wire (clothes-hanger wire will serve) are very useful. Wooden clothespins (clamp type) may be used wet, and there are many types of clamping devices which may be obtained from supply houses. So, make it fit!

Applying the flux   A small brush should be kept for applying the borax or handy flux to the metal to be soldered. When metal is heated, oxides form if the metal is not protected. The two fluxes suggested have a melting point just below that of easy-flow solder;

they work well for most soldering jobs by preventing oxidation at the temperatures required. So, flux the joint!

Selecting and preparing the solder We will use easy-flow, one of the three most common grades of silver solder. This solder, an alloy of silver, copper, and zinc, melts at 1280° F. and flows at 1325°, which provides an ample margin below the melting point of sterling silver (1640° F.). Both copper and brass have higher melting points, about 2000° and 1800° respectively.

Solder may be bought in wire or sheet form. Either works well, but wire is a little easier to clean and cut. To prepare wire solder, rub it with steel wool to remove oxides and cut it into small pieces (about $\frac{1}{16}$" long) with side nippers. Cut a few more pieces than are required into a piece of paper or a saucer. Then transfer the solder to the metal with a small brush or soldering poker dipped in flux. Place the pieces of solder about $\frac{1}{8}$" apart along the joint.

The amount of solder you use will depend upon your own working methods. Usually a very small amount will suffice. Craftsmen differ widely in their working techniques; some use larger quantities of solder and enough heat to make it flow over a larger area. This is especially true of craftsmen who started as silversmiths. Others use only enough solder to fill the joint and join the metals together. I advise beginning students to use only enough solder to do the job so that they will have less trouble with melting or burning the metals around the joint. As you gain more experience with heat control, you can use more solder.

Applying the heat Place the prepared object to be soldered on a fireproof surface—charcoal, asbestos, or a metal grille. Slowly preheat the metal, not the solder, until the water has dried out of the flux. If the solder moves, return it to its proper place with the soldering poker. After the water has boiled away, the flux will hold the solder in place until it flows. Continue heating the metal around the joint until it reaches a slight red color; the flux will again become liquid. At this point the heat may be concentrated on the joint until the solder flows. Remove the heat instantly when the solder flows; overheating weakens the joint and may burn the metal. If the solder balls up too much, heat is being applied to the solder, and the metal is not yet hot enough for the solder to flow. Solder flows to the hottest spot—a good reason for heating the larger pieces of metal first. With a little practice you can move the solder somewhat by controlling the heat.

If you encounter trouble, check your procedure. Often it is best to start all over. First check for *cleanliness;* second for *fit;* third for *flux* on all parts to be soldered; fourth, place the *solder* and then apply the heat.

PICKLING—REMOVING THE OXIDES, FLUX, AND DIRT

An acid cleaning solution made by mixing one (1) part of sulphuric to five (5) parts of water [always add the acid to the water] will remove the oxides formed when metals are heated. Sparex No. 2 may be used to replace the sulphuric acid; it will do the work of sulphuric acid without the danger. I advise its use especially when working in the home and with

handicapped people or with young children. It can
be used over and over again, and a one-pound can
costs only about 75¢ from most supply houses. The
acid solution will also remove the fire-hardened flux
that results from soldering. After the metal has lost
its red color but is still hot, it may be dropped into
the cold pickle solution. Many craftsmen use a weaker
solution, one part acid to ten parts water. This weaker
solution works more slowly and should be heated for
best results. With a stronger pickle solution only a
few minutes are required to remove the oxides from
the metal. In general, leave the silver in the pickling
solution until it turns white. After pickling, remove
the jewelry from the acid bath with wooden or copper
tongs and drop into water. Wash and dry the piece,
using a soft brush, soap, and water. If binding wire
or iron clamps have been used, be sure to remove
them before dipping the metal into the pickle. The
iron will contaminate the solution and will also dis-
color the silver if not removed. A half-water and half-
nitric-acid solution will remove oxides from silver,
but care must be observed: it works very fast and is
dangerous.

Instead of drying the washed piece of jewelry with
a cloth, many craftsmen use sawdust. Place the sawdust in a pan and heat it slightly on a stove or radi-
ator. The warm sawdust will dry the pieces quickly
and thoroughly without leaving lint or water marks
on the metal.

See *Bright Dip* in Chapter 3, page 38.

SOFT SOLDERING

For our purpose, soft solder is used primarily to
attach jewelry findings to pins, earrings, and other

jewelry. On some jewelry, however, soft solder is used for joining—especially on the cheap commercial type that is to be plated later. A small pencil soldering iron will provide enough heat for most soft soldering needs, since we only need about 400 to 500° of heat. To make soft-solder joints, clean the metal where a joint is desired, apply flux and a small amount of solder (more is required than silver solder)—too much solder is not good as it must be removed later. Apply only enough heat to melt the solder. Allow the solder and metal to cool before moving; then the piece may be dropped in pickle or water and cleaned, as instructed above. Most soft-solder fittings for jewelry have a small cup into which the solder may first be melted and later applied to the piece of jewelry by placing the finding in its proper position and reheating. This saves time when it comes to removing excess solder.

SWEAT SOLDERING

This term applies to the process of first tinning— applying a thin layer of solder to a metal that is to be soldered to another metal. This is usually used with sheet metals, as in appliqué work, but it can also be used to apply decorative wires to sheet metal. It is done by melting a thin layer of solder (hard or soft) onto the back of the metal and then reapplying flux. The piece of metal with the solder on it is clamped to the other metal, and heat applied until the solder flows to make a clean union. By watching carefully you can see the solder begin to flow at the edge of the metal.

FUSING METALS

One requirement for this type of work is an adequate heat source. A mouth pipe and city gas will suffice for small pieces, but by adding a foot bellows a better heat is obtained. A Bernz-o-matic or Propane burner will provide enough heat for small work, but I have found that for extensive work in fusing a Prest-o-lite tank is more satisfactory. Other materials needed are the scraps—pieces of silver, copper, and brass.

By checking the melting points of metals (given in this chapter) and by some experimenting, you will soon learn to get at least basic control of this process. A few suggestions to get you started should be all the help you need.

Try melting a few scraps of metal; remember that they tend to form into balls or drops because of surface tension. This is a working characteristic of metals. Check the color at various stages of the operation. This is the best guide or index in gaining control. Place a small piece of copper, brass, and silver —each coated with flux—beside each other on an asbestos pad and apply heat evenly to all three. The silver will become liquid and form a drop first (at about 1600°). The brass will melt next, and finally at about 2000° the copper will melt. This gives a working latitude of approximately 400°. Next, using a soldering poker made from a coat hanger or other heavy wire, push the pieces of metal together while they are hot. If they are still clean, they should adhere to each other and probably will combine to form a new alloy of the metals. If they do not, apply more heat and flux.

For the next experiment, take a few scraps of copper wire and sheet. Arrange them on the asbestos pad and apply flux at the points where the pieces overlap. Apply heat to the copper, using a small hot flame so that you can control the heat of the different sections or pieces. After the whole is heated to a dull red, concentrate the heat on a section where two pieces join. When the metal is hot enough it will begin to melt, and the two pieces will become one. This is the crucial point, and the heat must be moved or the metal may be burned or become a large molten glob.

You are now ready to proceed with the addition of other metals. Because copper melts at a higher temperature than brass I start the piece of jewelry with copper, getting the basic shape and structure established before adding the brass. Brass wire can be used as solder if the copper does not melt easily, or if you do not wish to run the risk of destroying an interesting shape by using higher temperatures. The brass scraps may be added in the same manner that the copper was fused—the only difference is the lower melting temperature. Remember to use flux to keep the oxides away from the metals when they are hot. From time to time it is advisable to drop the piece of jewelry into the pickle solution and clean with a wire brush or steel wool to see what you are getting. This will also disclose weak joints. Look at the piece from all directions; sometimes the back or underside may be better than the side on which you have been working.

Some bits and pieces from a scrap box combined, burned, and melted as in the next illustration.

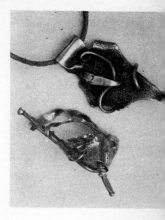

Notice the textural qualities obtained by burning the metal.

There is an enlightening little book called *The Creative Process,* edited by Brewster Ghiselin, which includes comments by many creative people in all branches of man's activities. You need only to check a few of the selections to recognize that most of man's discoveries were the result of an open-minded readiness to accept or see the significance or new relationships of whatever material they were working with. We must allow for a fresh examination of form and order as a guide to our own vital perception. Our jewelry then will be shaped by insight gained by the conscious activity which is a perceptive adjustment of materials and techniques to the desired end, a new and we hope interesting piece of decoration. It is never too early or late to start revitalizing your thinking and have fun in the process of creating your own jewelry. You have probably already recognized that this is the approach used by many modern painters and sculptors. More on this point in Chapter 9, where the major emphasis is design.

At the start you will have little control of the metal, but with practice a craftsman can exercise a great deal. For example, if you carve a shape into a charcoal block or fire brick, metal may be melted into that shape. (In short, this is a crude casting technique.)

Jewelry with real creative vitality can be produced by fusing various metals together. Exciting shapes and textures may be obtained by melting and burning the metals.

A piece of sterling jewelry combining burned and hammered surfaces.

Brass and copper often provide interesting, warm combinations with a stone or other materials. Sometimes it is better not to use silver. However, silver may be used at any time in the experiments; but once added, temperatures above 1600° should not be used, because the silver will melt and lose its shape. The metals may be used in all combinations or alone. By controlling the heat, both interesting shapes and also various textures can be produced. As you gain experience you will see many more possibilities.

The results of this process are largely dependent upon the ability of the craftsman to recognize beauty when he finds it. He begins to learn to utilize the accidental. On the other hand, the accidents are sought for and controlled. This jewelry can be refined and shaped by hammering and filing until the desired effect is obtained. It is difficult to plan for this type of work; it should be spontaneous and expressive of the materials and the technique. It has been said many times and in many ways that "Beauty is where you find it." This is the key to the door of discovery. Keep an open mind. Be ready to use the good and discard or modify the less interesting results.

As you experiment you will find new and interesting shapes developing which, when combined with other shapes, can prove very exciting. If you will look

Hammered and formed metal are integrated with fused parts in a combination of sterling silver and brass.

Many small scraps were combined in this first piece of jewelry made by a librarian. The stone, a piece of polished obsidian found on a trip in Mexico, is held within the fused metal. Both front and back of the piece are shown to illustrate the whole construction of the pendant.

around, you will find other materials—beach pebbles, shells, driftwood, and many others—that can be combined with the metal. With a little planning, prongs may be added to secure the various materials. Since wood, stones, and similar materials will not withstand heat, do not fasten them until you have completed all the work that involves heat.

If you have learned how metals react to heat and have learned to solder, you are ready to move on to some other basic operations.

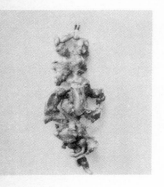

A moss agate is held in this baroque con-struction of fused metals. It can be worn as a pendant or a brooch.

A seashell provides the contrast in this con-struction of partially fused metals.

This delicate arrangement of fused wire and scraps of silver and brass holds a piece of petrified wood.

5 * CUTTING, DRILLING, AND PIERCING SHEET METALS

* *

The jeweler's saw is the basic cutting tool for the metal craftsman, although time can often be saved by using cutting shears of various kinds. These cutting devices range in size from the small household scissors used to cut metal foil through metal snips to the large bench shears (similar to a paper cutter) designed to make either straight or curved cuts. I know of no shears that can make inside cuts; these must be done with a saw, and the process is referred to as *piercing* or *saw-piercing*. Motor-driven jigsaws in which jeweler's saw blades may be clamped are adaptable to the cutting of metals, but for most hand craftsmen the jeweler's saw remains the most essential cutting tool.

* Tools

Jeweler's saw frame   2½″ throat adequate for most jewelry work, but for larger pieces a 4″ throat is needed, so get the larger one.

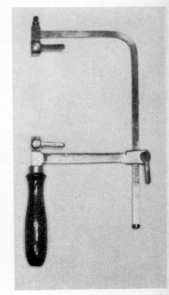

Adjustable jeweler's saw frame with clamping device to hold the small jeweler's-saw blades.

61

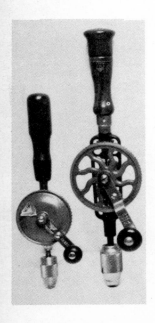

Jeweler's saw blades	Size 2/0 small for thin metal 22 gauge or thinner. Size 1 medium for general work.
Wiss shears	A fine cutting tool developed for the aircraft industry, which is finding ready acceptance by many silversmiths and jewelers. May be obtained from most hardware stores. I find I use it almost to the exclusion of all other shears.
Diagonal cutters	6" size for cutting wire. (Shears should not be used to cut wire.)
Leather mallet	To flatten metal when bent.
Hand drill Small drills	May be obtained from all hardware and department stores.
Wax	Beeswax or a wax candle will work nicely to reduce friction on the saw.
Flexible-shaft machine	Used by most professional jewelers. The accuracy, versatility, and speed provided by this tool is well worth the cost—about $35 plus attachments. (This is something for later work but if you already have one, use it.)

✱ *Materials*

Copper, brass, and sterling silver are available in standard gauges. Below are some of the ones used most often by craftsmen. Unless you specify otherwise, all sterling is annealed or soft when you buy it, and copper, brass, and bronze may be obtained annealed. If you buy silver in quantities of 5 ounces or more you will realize a considerable saving. Check your supplier's catalogue for sizes. If you don't have

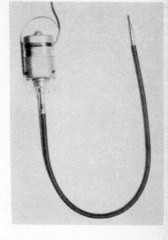

Top: flexible shaft tool. Center: handpieces for the flexible-shaft tool. Bottom: a few of the many cutting, grinding, and polishing tools used in the flexible-shaft tool. Your dentist's drills will work and he will probably give you his old ones.

a catalogue, write for one now. (Check the appendix for addresses.)

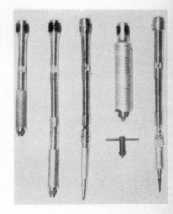

B & S Gauge	
36-gauge metal foil	Best for beginning experiments
24	
22	Used for earrings, pins, brooches,
20	beads, buttons, and bezels.
18	Good for lightweight modeled and
16	pierced designs.
14	Used for rings, bracelets, pendants
12	and for heavy forged or pierced
	designs.

Circles may be obtained in the above gauges in sizes ranging from about ½″ to 6″. They provide interesting experimental devices and save time. Foil can be purchased in brass, copper, and the common aluminum foil used by the cook; all work well for experiments.

CUTTING SHEET WITH SHEARS

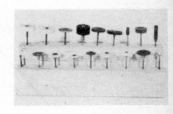

If you've cut paper or cloth with scissors, you know how to cut metal. The shears are bigger and the metal tougher. Simply hold the shears at a right angle to the metal, which is pushed against the cutting edges with the left hand while the right operates the shears. Guiding the cut is a combined process of both hands; sometimes the metal is moved, but more often the direction of the shears is changed.

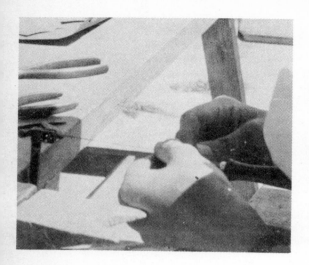

By placing the saw against the worktable, pressure may be exerted by pressing forward with the chest while the blade is clamped into the sawframe. Clamp one end, then the other. Broken blades may be used by adjusting the sawframe.

Small circles are usually stamped out with a circle cutter on a wood or lead block.

SAWING

Place the saw blade in the frame as shown in the illustration; keep the blade taut with the saw teeth pointing toward the handle. This is necessary since the actual cutting action is done on the down stroke. Hold the saw lightly but firmly in a vertical position so that an easy up-and-down motion can be achieved. By holding the piece to be sawed against a V-notched bench pin, the entire sawing operation may be accomplished with ease. Very small pieces of metal may be held with the aid of a ring clamp, hand vise, or a pair of pliers while sawing.

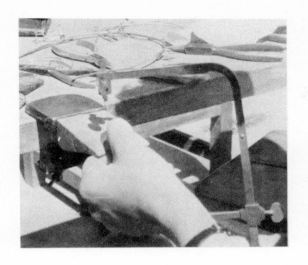

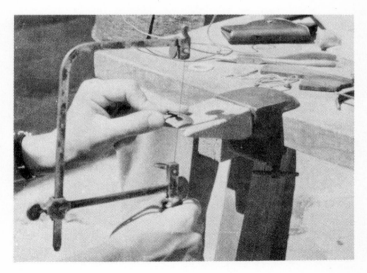

Close-up of saw-piercing operation using V block to facilitate holding the metal to be sawed.

EXPERIMENTS IN CUTTING AND DRILLING·

Let's start with some experiments made in such thin metals as copper or aluminum foil. We are looking for ideas and learning as we play. A completely relaxed attitude is most conducive to this type of work. The metal may be cut with simple household scissors and requires very little strength. You may prefer heavier gauges, which have the advantage of strength and may be used as the final jewelry, although the foils may often be used if they are reinforced to add sufficient durability. The gauge or thickness of the metal is not too important. It is not wrong to use 20-gauge rather than 22- or 18-gauge. If it looks right, it *is* right. Make a few cuts to get the feel of the process—some straight cuts, some round cuts, a free cut circle, and some free forms. Look at the cuts, but look at both the negative and the positive shapes you have obtained. Try duplicating the cuts and forms; repeat them in different sizes. You are working for variety, and the free play of thought serves to release the tensions set up by trying to force yourself to invent or create a given order. The discipline of conscious control will grow naturally as you strive for simple, expressive forms. The very struggle of consciously looking for new forms, shapes, and the complexity behind a simple organization is extremely rewarding and satisfying. When you abandon the results of your efforts and go on to the next challenge, though it may be similar, you are still seeking the "right" solution to your problem. From these free explorations with tools, techniques, and materials, fundamentals will come into focus, and you add to your experience discoveries from which you can build solutions for specific projects.

So far we have been using scissors or metal shears. Now try the jeweler's saw. Any metal thicker than 24 gauge will work. Notice the difference between the edges made by cutting devices. Which gives you better control? Make with the saw some cuts that cannot be made with shears. How do they differ? Recently I met a goldsmith who told me that he uses the saw with the teeth pointing away from the handle for many cutting operations, although all books and most craftsmen advocate placing the blade in the saw with the teeth pointing toward the handle. This is good advice for the beginner, but can we improve techniques by blindly following a set pattern? Think first, "what do I want to do?" The method or technique will naturally follow.

A form or shape may need a hole or cutout space inside its area. Try a hand drill or the flexible-shaft

A Swiss-cheese friendship ring illustrating holes drilled at various angles.

machine and make a few different-sized holes. Start the hole by making a small dent in the metal with a center punch or nail. This will locate the hole and provide a start for the drill. Drill the holes straight by holding the drill at a right angle to the metal to be drilled. Now try some at different angles. Notice how the round hole is no longer round but rather oval in shape; the sides of the hole, especially in thicker metal, change as the position of our eye changes. Place a saw blade through a hole and attach the saw frame; saw from one hole to another, holding the metal firmly against the V in the bench pin.

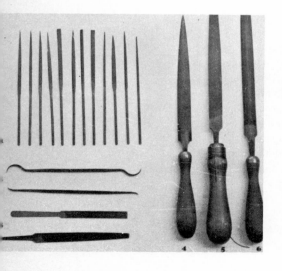

The most useful files used in jewelry-making.

FILING

Naturally some of these experimental cuts will be rough. If a smooth edge is desired, they may be filed to remove the rough spots. The curve may be improved or a line made straight as desired. To get into corners and inside areas, use a needle file of the correct cross section for the shape you want.

CREATING JEWELRY FROM THE EXPERIMENTS

Remember what was done with wire in the first chapter. Use a similar approach here to organize various parts. Now is a good time to try some appliqué work, discussed more fully in Chapter 7. Sweat-solder several of your pieces together. Use some of your shot for accents. Arrange and rearrange—more on this later after a few more techniques are acquired—but if you want to finish some of the experiments or continue to work in this method, look over the section on design, where you will find more suggestions. To attach findings, review the section on jewelry findings (page 25) if you haven't already solved this problem to your own satisfaction.

A tie slide using cut metal and wire appliqué. The slide was oxidized and only the high spots were polished to create the contrast.

A simple sawed-and-drilled design soldered to a similar back shape.

Finished examples of saw-pierced work indicating use of positive and negative shapes.

6 * SHAPING, HAMMERING, AND PLANISHING (SHEET METALS)

* *

Now let's add a third dimension to our experiments with sheet metal. True, when two surfaces overlap, the third dimension is introduced, but now the object here is consciously to work for three-dimensional arrangements. Metal may be formed and shaped in many ways. A surface may be flat, concave, or convex, or have combinations of the three. Most of the work of raising or lowering a surface is done with hammers or mallets over metal or wooden forms. The jewelry metal may be forced into depressions made in wood or metal blocks with a hammer or with dapping dies. Many interesting surfaces and textures may be produced on the metal surface.

* Tools

Ball peen hammer (about 8 oz.)
Rawhide mallet (1¼" x 2½")

All that we need, but others may prove useful. See illustration.

Some of the hammers and mallets found in most jewelry shops.

71

Dapping blocks and dies used to make domes and half-spheres. They are produced in various sizes for variety of scale.

Wood blocks—hardwood is better—old sections of trees work well.

Metal blocks and stakes—come in many shapes and sizes—consult your dealers' catalogues.

Dapping block—used to make domes and spheres—a very useful tool.

Lead block—useful for pounding depressions into metal.

Sandbag

Vise

Pliers

* *Materials* The materials are the same used in the last chapter. In fact, you should experiment with at least some of the shapes already made and kept in your "Idea Box."

EXPERIMENTING

Take a piece of foil or other light metal about 6″ × 6″. The size isn't important, as long as it is large enough to give you ample opportunity to work it. See how many ways you can mutilate the metal. Cut it, bend it, pound it, twist it. How many ways did you find? Check what others have done—have they thought of any other ways? Compare the results. Do they suggest new and unusual possibilities? This is not to make jewelry, but to gain confidence, to understand the properties of the metals, their strengths and limitations, and to release your fears of a new material.

All base metals (copper, gold, and silver) are soft

and ductile. They may be stretched and pushed around fairly easily. Repeated hammer blows in an area cause a depression in the metal, or if the metal is hammered over a hard surface, it will take the form of that surface. One side becomes convex, the other concave. Either one may be used for jewelry. Sometimes, the metal is pounded into a depression—the dapping block, for example—which produces a dome or half-sphere. Free-form depressions are pounded into a lead block or carved into a wooden block and the metal may then be pounded into them. Many kinds of stakes are available for use as forms to shape metals, and many forms may be improvised by using hammers, dapping dies, or other pieces of metal held in a vise. The metal is then shaped around the stake for the desired shape or form. A rawhide mallet will not mark the metal; if you desire a smooth surface on the metal, its use is advisable.

Don't overlook pliers as a forming tool. Many bends, angles, and other shapes may be created simply by forming the metal in the jaws of various pliers. A spiral shape may be made by wrapping a strip of metal around a pair of round-nose pliers, and a simple and effective earring results. The clip part of a tie bar may be made in the manner shown at right, or it may be bent around a nail held in a vise. Zigzag surfaces are made by alternating the direction of the clamping of the pliers. You will think of other twists, bends, and manipulations to produce other forms. (See also the section on models in Chapter 9.)

Many textural qualities may be produced by using various hammers. A ball-peen hammer makes a round dent in the metal, and when many such dents are combined a rough surface results. The size of the

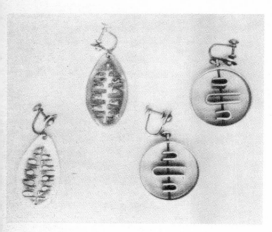

Examples of jewelry for which hammer and pliers were utilized as forming devices. Left: earring shapes made with pliers as forming tools. The pair on the left was sawed, the prongs bent forward and the ends fused or melted. The right-hand pair was formed entirely with pliers. Below: two pins with the same shape but different textures. Below left: a pendant formed by cutting the metal and then shaping with pliers to create a concave effect, and bottom: two pendants formed using a lead block into which the metal was hammered. The pendant on the left provides nice contrast of smooth and pierced surfaces.

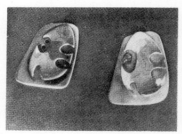

dent is determined by the force of the stroke and
the flatness or roundness and size of the hammer
used. A cross-peen or riveting hammer gives an
inverted U-shaped dent, and other hammers produce other types of surface. When this type of surface is antiqued, the high spots polished, a very
decorative texture is obtained. If such a surface is
used in combination with a smooth surface, many
interesting contrasts may result and introduce variety.

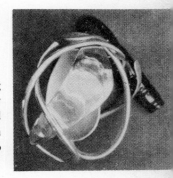

PLANISHING

Metal may be made smooth simply by hammering
it. This is a silversmithing technique, but it is very
useful on small pieces of jewelry. After the desired
shape is obtained, there will be hammer marks on
the surface and the surface itself may be irregular. To

*A convertible and detachable bracelet that
that can be worn as individual pieces or
in several combinations. The sheet-metal
part of the bracelet illustrates a highly
polished surface obtained by planishing.*

*The sail-like shapes
in this pin–pendant
were planished and
polished before be-
ing soldered to-
gether.*

remove these tool marks and to true the surface, use a planishing hammer with a relatively flat face. By hitting the metal carefully with light but firm strokes the surface of the metal will be smoothed out until few or no marks are left. This is actually easier than filing the surface. The piece is then finished as suggested in Chapter 3.

An interesting bird form produced by a student who used only pliers for the forming operations, a pendant that makes use of a domed circle to provide a setting for a fire opal, and earrings of roughly hammered bent wire.

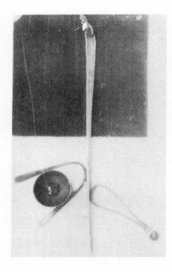

7 * DECORATING TECHNIQUES: APPLIQUÉ, STAMPING, CHASING, REPOUSSÉ AND ETCHING

✳ ✳ ✳ ✳ ✳ ✳ ✳ ✳ ✳ ✳ ✳ ✳ ✳ ✳ ✳ ✳ ✳ ✳ ✳

This section limits itself to some simple techniques. There are other books that cover this area in greater detail; refer to them when you are ready for more information. (See Bibliography.) Engraving, for example, requires a great deal of skill and is a highly specialized field. Few hand jewelers do their own engraving, preferring to have it done by professional engravers. If you are interested and have three or four months to practice, even as an average craftsman you can develop the ability to engrave.

We will investigate briefly ways of making lines and raising small areas—in short, ways to decorate our jewelry. The processes covered here are all relatively easy, but allow a wide variety of applications.

✳ Tools

Jeweler's saw	You already have all of these
Hammer or mallet	
Side or diagonal nippers	
Files	
Pliers	
Hardwood or metal block	
Lead block	

77

Metal stamps (See Appendix B: Tools)	You can make these with nails or tool steel by filing and hammering; most supply houses have them
Chasing tools (See figure at left)	Liners, planishers, and punches are the basic ones. Others may be added later.

* *Materials*

Metal foil
Wire of various gauges

Sheet metals	16 to 20 gauge—copper or sterling is best, depending upon size and type of design; 16 gauge is good for bracelets.
Masking tape	or other acid resistant such as asphaltan or resist varnish
Nitric acid	
Equipment for cleaning	oxidizing and finishing
Sketch book	

The purpose of this section is to discover some of the decorative possibilities and to allow more freedom of expression in your jewelry. They may be used separately or in combination.

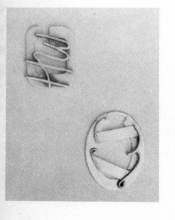

APPLIQUÉ

When wire or sheet-metal forms are soldered onto the surface of another metal form, the process is usually referred to as *appliqué*. Two or three layers or plates of different metals may be used, and wire may be integrated into the design to provide lines where desired. Negative shapes are produced by saw-piercing and may be used on any or all layers. Often the cutout shape provides an interesting design element when soldered above the cutout area.

You have already learned all the techniques required for this type of work: cutting, piercing, filing, soldering, and finishing. Now you can concentrate more on the designing, but the technique you use will influence the type of design you will make.

Briefly, here is the procedure: cut out the forms from sheet metal, or form wire into the design you want. After the forms meet your approval and are cleaned, solder them to the backplate of your design. When copper is used, sweat soldering reduces the amount of clean-up required. Always use a minimum of solder if it will show, or try to integrate it into the design.

First, two-dimensional shapes work well, but very interesting effects may be obtained when the shapes are bent and formed, creating three-dimensional jewelry. Bracelets, pins, brooches, tie bars, or any other type jewelry may be produced.

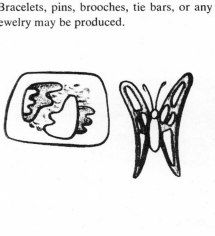

STAMPING

Much Indian and Mexican jewelry is produced in this manner; various types of stamps are available. Often such jewelry is crude and poorly designed, but the process itself is not at fault. Stamping may be used to create interesting textures and surface qualities if the jeweler uses his ingenuity as a craftsman.

Stamps may be made from nails or tool steel simply by cutting the nail with a saw and filing it smooth. This will produce a round ● stamp. The head of a nail will produce a larger circle. By drilling an indentation in the end of the cut-off nail a ◯ stamp may be made. To create a shape ／ the nail is pounded flat, cut, and smoothed. Other shapes are produced by filing the ends of nails into the shapes you want—triangles, ovals, cones, and diamonds. These stamps are similar to those used in leather decoration. In fact, for metal foils, the leather tools may be used.

These shapes may be thought of as basic shapes or elements of design. To create decorations or patterns, repeat or alternate the motifs in an area or as

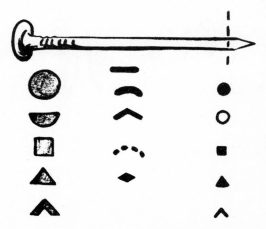

an all-over pattern. After you have obtained or made
a few stamps, try them out on a piece of metal foil
placed on a steel plate. Do not pound too hard or
you will cut through the metal. Tap lightly with a
hammer; one sharp clean blow works best. Also,
try stamps on a soft surface such as a lead block or
a pad of newspaper.

For examples of this type of work, look at Indian
jewelry and leather work. Better, strike out on your
own and see how inventive you can be.

CHASING AND REPOUSSÉ

Chasing thin metal is a very easy process. Common sense and patience will insure a fair degree of
success. With thin metals the use of chasing tools
is not required. Simple clay-modeling or leather-work-
ing tools will suffice, or you can make your own by
filing a smooth round or spoon-shaped end on a nail.
A burnishing tool will also serve nicely. If you wrap
some tape around the nail or drive it into a section
of broom handle or dowel rod, you will have a grip
that will facilitate handling it.

Chasing is done on the front of the metal by forcing
the metal in. Any such surface as a blotter, cardboard, or lead block will provide a working surface. Repoussé, meaning "thrust back," is done from
the back surface of the metal. By combining the two
techniques, you can depress or raise lines and areas
as you wish.

Try a few lines on some scraps of metal foil, working only on the front. Next, try to depress several
areas. Now turn the metal over and work from the
back. Buttons and other jewelry may be made in this

way. Filling the back of the metal with sealing wax or plaster of Paris adds strength and durability. Jewelry findings may be glued or soldered to the back. Although this is not truly chasing or repoussé, it will give you the feel of the process and will introduce you to the design possibilities of the technique.

Real chasing or repoussé is done with chasing tools, with the metal held in pitch for better control. Lines are made with liners or tracers. Embossing or forming tools are used to raise the metal and smoothing or planishing is done with planishers. Other specialized tools produce a wide variety of effects. The actual working of the surface is done by holding the tool lightly in the left hand to guide it as it is struck with a light chasing hammer. This tool has a thin-necked handle to give it spring for rapid hammering. A lead block furnishes a satisfactory backing for many chas-

An example of Mexican repoussé and cut black onyx jewelry.

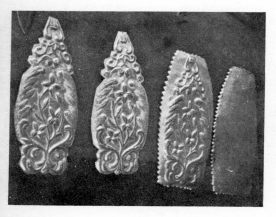

An example of chasing repoussé that shows several steps in the process. The jagged edges on the two stages provide a holding device when placed in the pitch. Part of the metal was first worked from the front, reversed on the pitch, and then worked from the reverse side.

The central portion of these earrings was etched using a simple wax resist.

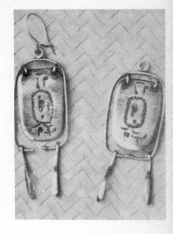

ing projects, but pitch is the ideal compound. To adhere the metal, warm the pitch with a torch until it gets soft and sticky, then press the metal lightly into the pitch. To remove, heat the pitch and metal and remove with pliers or tweezers. Any pitch that sticks to the metal should be burned off or dissolved with kerosene. Afterward drop the metal into the pickle and clean as discussed before.

ETCHING

Acid will etch or eat away metals if they are not protected. By applying some material that will resist acid and exposing only part of the metal, we can control the action of the acid. The exposed areas will be depressed, the protected areas will remain in relief. Usually a resist varnish or asphaltum is used to protect the metal, but a simple resist may be improvised by using Scotch or masking tape. Simply apply a thin layer of tape to the metal, and uncover the areas to be etched by removing the tape over them with a sharp knife. Shapes may be cut from the tape and applied to the metal, and after etching they will remain in relief. Or use candle or beeswax as an acid resist. Warm the metal and coat it by rubbing a candle over the surface, or melt the wax and apply it with a brush. Lines and areas may then be scratched through the wax so that the acid will reach the metal. Remember to protect all areas (including the back) that do not require etching.

When the design is ready, place the metal into a solution of about ⅓ nitric acid and ⅔ water (add acid to water slowly) in a glass container. Check the etching action every few seconds. If the solution is working properly, the metal exposed to the acid will be covered with many small gas bubbles. If you desire a smoothly etched surface, brush the bubbles off the metal with a feather or a brush made of string. A pebble effect will result if the bubbles are not removed. Choose your effect. When the desired depth of etch is reached, usually about ⅓ the thickness of the metal, remove the jewelry from the acid, remove the resist, and clean and polish as before. Do not inhale the fumes from the etching solution. Remember that acid is dangerous when used carelessly.

Now that you have experimented with these techniques, you realize some of their design potential. You can apply them to any kind of jewelry and in any combination. The variation and application are entirely of your own choosing and are determined by your own approach to jewelry.

8 * STONES AND STONE SETTING

* *

Stones suitable for jewelry may be found in your own back yard. They may not be precious, but who cares? Select them for their interesting shapes or colors. Of course some areas are better and offer more variety, but consult local "rockhounds" to see how many varieties of semiprecious stones and mineral specimens are at hand for the picking. Each year the spring issue of *Lapidary Journal* includes a "Rockhound Buyers Guide," "Annual Encyclopedia," "Treasure Trails," and lists many dealers of cut and uncut materials in all parts of the country. This is such a good source of up-to-date information that you will find a few hours of perusing it both fascinating and rewarding.

Another fine guide for collecting and identifying stones is the 1958 edition of *Getting Acquainted with Minerals,* revised by David E. Jensen. Mr. Jensen, who is head of the Geological Division of Wards' Natural Science Establishment, has been very helpful with students of jewelry. My own classes have been visiting Wards in Rochester, N.Y., for many years; they have always been able to obtain many interesting specimens of tumble-polished semipre-cious stones, uncut crystals, and various minerals at very reasonable prices. You may have such a source of materials in your own area, or you can order from Wards, Allcraft, or other supply houses by mail. Most reputable dealers will send consignments of stones from which you can select what you want and return the rest. In this chapter we will concern our-selves primarily with providing settings for the stones.

There is probably more romance, superstition, and fascination woven about precious stones than any other substance that man uses. Precious stones and precious metals go together like love and kisses. As far back as we can trace we find jewels playing an important part in world history. Certain stones were used in many symbolic ways, and some still maintain their significance.

A few generalizations here may be helpful to the beginning craftsman to aid him in making his selec-tions. For more precise information consult any of the stone buyers guides or encyclopedias.

One of the first factors to consider is the relative hardness of the gem stone. The Mohs' scale, used in high school science courses, applies here. One (1) represents talc, which is very soft; the scale progresses in hardness to 10, or diamond, the hardest substance. Since dust or sand has a hardness of about 7, it is advisable to use stones above that degree of hardness. However, several very popular stones—including opal, turquoise, moonstone, and lapis—are softer and scratch easily. Pearls are only about 2½ to 3½ on the scale, yet they maintain their popularity and price. Topaz, jade, garnet, corundum (ruby and sapphire), quartz (amethyst, jasper, carnelian, and onyx), and the beryls (emerald and aquamarine), as well as diamonds, are all harder. When a softer stone is used, it should be protected from wear and scratches.

The color of a gem is also important, but very misleading as a means of identification, as there are several gem stones that occur in nearly all colors. (Usually the more rare the color they are, the more expensive.) However, many of the most beautiful colors are the most common, and therefore less expensive. Many nice stones may be obtained for prices ranging from about 50¢ to $10.

From the jewelery craftsman's point of view, the shape may be the most important factor to consider. You may select a stone and then build the design around it, or you may make a design and then get the stone. To start, the first procedure is better, since the stone itself may suggest the design and structure of the piece. The most common styles or shapes of cut stones are faceted (for transparent and semitransparent stones) and cabochon (bald-head) for opaque gems, cuts which bring out their color and luster. Uncut crystals and fragments along with the tumbled or free-form stones have been popular for the last few years, and they will probably maintain that popularity in the future.

SOME EASY SETTINGS

* *Trapped, wrapped, and caged* Free-form tumbled and uncut semiprecious gem stones provide many interesting possibilities. Don't worry about involved

Simple cages to hold a variety of beach stones or polished baroque stones.

equipment or techniques. Simply capture or hold the stones in cradles of wire. Sterling is excellent, but copper and brass wire can be used and are actually better for some stones. You don't need a workshop; in fact, you could work in bed to produce traps and cages for the stones. All you need is a pair of pliers and wire nippers, wire of various gauges (12 or 14 gauge for heavy stones or frames, and 16 to 20 for lacing or caging). Use your fingers first, to get the general shapes, then make the refinements with the pliers. Be sure the stone is held securely and crimp or twist the wire tight with your pliers where necessary. All types of jewelry can be made in this manner.

There are many variations to this basic type of trapping. Let the stone suggest the procedure. Often stones have flaws that need to be protected or even covered. Think of a fishnet and how the fish are caught as they try to escape. The spider web may suggest an approach for you. Look at the roots of trees in rocky soil; see how organically they grasp the rocks. Just begin and your ingenuity and imagination will do the rest.

While this technique produces interesting jewelry, you can also refine the process by applying what you have already learned. Hammer the wire to create better relationships of line and form. Reduce the amount of wire to allow the stone to show all its color and beauty. With solder (remove the stone) better and more interesting forms that repeat the essential form of the stone may be produced. Other materials

Polished tiger's eye trapped in a spiral of wire to create a pin.

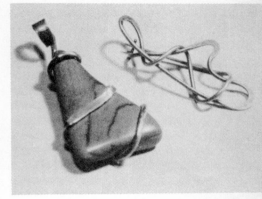

Earrings in which square sterling wire holds an amethyst polished by tumbling, and a copper pendant with a beach pebble.

Rutilated quartz trapped in silver to form a pendant.

Top: two views of a pin–pendant using half-round sterling silver wire. The work was completed by the addition of a pin back and a hanging loop. Below: two views of a pendant using a minimum of silver.

Earrings to match the pendant above.

such as wood, bones, horn, and seedpods may also be used. (See the section on combinations, page 127.)

* *Simple wire settings* These settings may be made from a few lengths of wire arranged and soldered for a durable method of holding the stone. The sketches are meant to suggest some of the possibilities, but you will think of others. The prongs may be hammered and filed to fit the shape of the stone.

They may be used for all shapes of stones, cut or uncut, and for all kinds of jewelry by attaching to findings you make or buy.

* *Simple sheet-metal settings* Here is another easy way of holding stones; it, too, provides many design possibilities. This technique, using 18- or 20-gauge metal, holds the stones by means of prongs or clamps

Any shape—beach stones, crystals, seed pods, sea shells, etc.—may be held with wire. By soldering wire units together both variety and strength can be added to the setting.

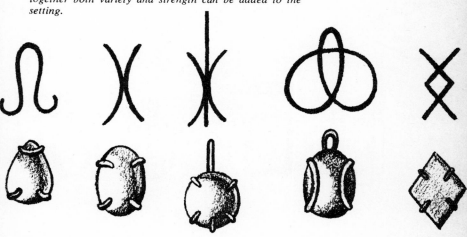

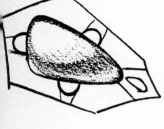

which are cut with shears or a jeweler's saw. Place the stone on a piece of metal—a scrap will work and may suggest other ideas; draw around the stone; then draw the prongs as shown at the left. Cut out the resulting shape and force the prongs around the stone with pliers or a burnisher.

You probably already see other variations to this technique, but here are a few to keep your imagination working. For example, cut out a shape in metal the exact size and shape or a little larger than the stone. Now turn the stone. You will have clamps to fold up over the stone to hold it in place. (See sketch.) This may be done with wire also. For another technique, draw around a stone placed on a piece of metal; now drill a hole in the center of the metal. Using a jeweler's saw, make eight cuts out to the edge of the stone. This will provide eight prongs. Bend every other one forward, and you have a setting for your stone.

A basic method of using sheet metal to provide settings for all stones including the popular baroque.

Variations suggesting other possibilities for sheet metal will be found in these illustrations.

✳ *Bezel settings* This type of setting is probably the best and most durable because it protects the stone from all but the most severe shocks. Most stones, even the hardest diamond, fracture or chip easily when struck a sharp blow. I had to replace the rubies in a ring twice during the war because I kept cracking them on the controls of the aircraft I was flying. You may have had similar experiences, so with better stones take every precaution for their protection. Since the bezel protects the stone on all sides except the face, it provides more protection.

Bezel settings may be roughly classified into two basic types, the *box* and the *bearing,* which are used for cabochon and step-cut stones. A box setting is used when the back of the stone is flat. A simple band of metal, the size of the stone, is made, soldered and then soldered to a backplate. If the stone back is

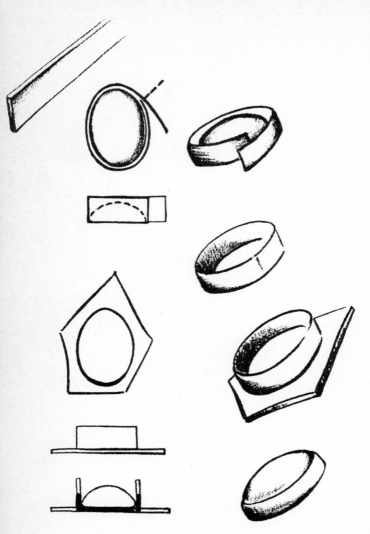

Reading from top to bottom, the basic technique of making a bezel setting is illustrated. Starting with a strip of 26- or 28-gauge silver, sizing it to the stone, and finally attaching it to a backing demonstrates the complete process.

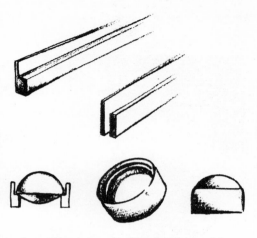

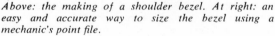

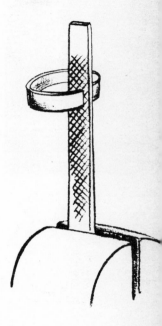

Above: the making of a shoulder bezel. At right: an easy and accurate way to size the bezel using a mechanic's point file.

curved, some provision must be made to accommodate the projection. This is done by using a prepared bearing bezel, or you may make one by shaping a shoulder upon which the stone can rest. (See sketches.) I suggest starting with oval or round stones.

Twenty-six- or 28-gauge sterling may be used, but fine silver is better for student work because it is softer and melts at a higher temperature. Since the metal is very thin, it will melt quickly when too much heat is used, so you must be careful when applying the torch. It is advisable to make the bezel higher than is actually needed for the stone. After all soldering is completed, it should be filed away before the stone is set. The bezel must be high enough to hold the stone securely.

Striped agate set with a bezel soldered to a backpiece.

Bracelet of wire units and a bezel-set stone.

Cufflinks using a bezel without a back.

* *Procedure in brief* Wrap a thin piece of metal around the stone and cut it to size. It should be snug but not tight. A small flat file such as a mechanic's point file works well for final sizing of the bezel. Clamp it in a bench vise in a vertical position. By placing one end of the bezel on each side of the file and using an up-and-down motion, both ends may be filed at the same time to insure a fit. (See sketch.) When the bezel fits the stone, solder the two ends together, making a ring. Place the ring on a backplate; any scrap larger than the ring will do. The gauge of metal is determined by the size of the stone. After the ring and backplate are soldered, cut and file the backplate to size. When all soldering and the rough filing and shaping are completed, place the stone in the bezel, and push the metal up against the stone with a stone setter or burnisher. Do not move the tool around the stone, but rather use a rolling, up-and-over motion to push the metal against the stone. I find it is a good idea to place the left thumb over the stone to help prevent slips of the tool. Work all sides of the metal; do not concentrate on one side. Sometimes the center of the backplate is cut away to allow light to reach the back of the stone.

If a bearing bezel is used, the shoulder replaces the backplate. To make a bezel for a ring, the shoulder must be high enough to allow filing the back of the bezel to the shape of the finger or ring shank. (See sketch.)

The use of a half-round file in fitting a bezel setting to a ring shank.

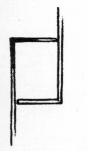

A rectangular stone can be set by using the methods of filing and folding illustrated at the left.

Bezels for rectangular stones must be fitted very carefully. They may be made in one piece by filing a nick about ¾ of the way through the metal at each corner. They are reinforced with solder when the two ends are soldered. It is easiest to get a good fit by using two pieces of metal as shown in sketch. Cut the ends off after they are soldered together.

✳ *Prong settings*   Commercial jewelers use many types of prong settings. They may be simple or complex. Here is a simple procedure that provides the basic knowledge for setting stones in this manner. This setting is especially good for facet-cut stones, but is sometimes also used for cabochon-cut stones. One major advantage of this setting is that it allows light to get to nearly the entire stone and thus enhance the fire or color of the gem.

First, make a base of wire for the stone to rest upon. (See right.) The outside edge should be the exact size of the stone's girdle. Next, cut the prongs from round, square, half-round, or rectangular wire of proper gauge—usually about 14. Make them longer than the stone requires. After the base is soldered, make small file marks on its outside edge where the prongs will be soldered. Place the base on a charcoal block and push the prongs into the block in their proper position. The charcoal will hold them in place while they are being soldered. After soldering cut and file the excess wire away.

The number of prongs and the thickness and shape of the base are determined by the stone's shape and

size. For small round stones three prongs work well,
but for square or larger stones four or more prongs
are necessary. Sometimes the prongs are joined together below the stones, as in the sketch, to create a
base which can then be soldered to the piece. Prong
settings for transparent stones with faceted surfaces
require considerable skill and patience, but they can
be constructed in a similar manner. Often they are
made from sheet by first constructing a cone which
is later cut and filed to shape. A simple prong setting
of this type is a variation of the simple sheet-metal
settings already discussed.

When to use a particular type of setting must be
decided by the craftsman and depends on which type
best suits both the stone and the piece of jewelry. By
now you know enough about the metal, its limitations
and potentials, and you have developed enough skill
in the basic techniques, to do what you want. More
experience will of course improve these techniques.
You may discover better and easier ways to obtain
the results you want in your own way.

We have mentioned design, form, and function as
we progressed through these basic techniques; now
we will concentrate on these aspects of the problem.

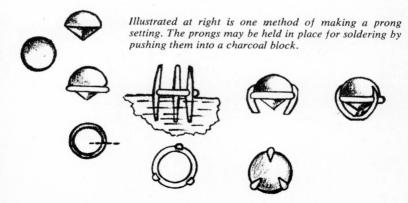

*Illustrated at right is one method of making a prong
setting. The prongs may be held in place for soldering by
pushing them into a charcoal block.*

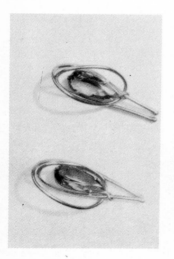

Top left: rings using bezel and prong settings. Top right: simple prong-and-bezel settings. Left: prong settings in gold and topaz earrings, and below, prongs used to hold a shell in an oval of braided wire.

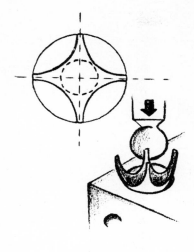

A .dapping block adds variety of method to making sheet-metal prong settings (below). At right is a method . of making prongs using a cone.

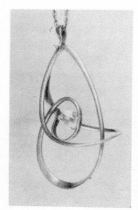

Parts of and a completed "Sputnik" bracelet.

A wire setting for a "Herkimer" diamond.

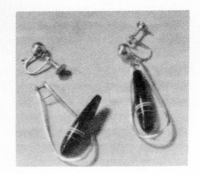

Top left: tie clip; above, striped agate drops held in sterling earrings, and left, a pendant.

9 ✳ FORM AND FUNCTION

✳ ✳

DESIGN

In good design, art is so closely linked with structure that it merges with and sometimes replaces the structural elements. The object, in this case the piece of jewelry to be made, is held in a triangle of forces: first, materials, tools, and processes; second, form (the total plastic organization); third, use or function,· including the psychological function. This may be simply diagramed as below.

There is no *best* design. You cannot be certain how to design something well, but you *can* be certain how to design it poorly. If it goes counter to the triangle above, you can be sure that what you make is bad.

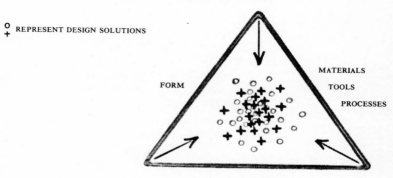

o
+ REPRESENT DESIGN SOLUTIONS

FORM

MATERIALS

TOOLS

PROCESSES

FUNCTION

It is relatively easy to determine when a thing is bad. But what is "good"? In this sense, good is related to perfection—which in turn is made up of many little things. But perfection is itself no little thing; perfection is unobtainable, but a goal well worth striving toward.

Our pioneer industries, those which deal with new products, materials, and problems (for example aircraft, rockets, and missiles) create a unity of appreciation and emphasize the principle that no design can be made or judged in isolation from others. Although the products of these industries are not yet hampered by history and tradition, they imply that the important element in design is shape (form). Our preoccupation with form is a new and radical approach to the world about us that is not confined to any art but applies to our whole culture. Science today is concerned with relation, structure, and shape, while a hundred years ago it was concerned with exact measurement. Today we hardly ask how large space is, but rather is it open or closed on itself? In our society we express logical relations as structure, and we express structure in terms of shape or form. In the past we had a positive approach to right and wrong, true or false. Victorian esthetics were positive; ours are more organic and experimental.

What is it that impresses you when you see something you consider beautiful? It is the interrelation of parts, to each other and to the whole, which constitutes beauty as seen by the eye, be it a Miss America, a rose, an airplane, or a piece of jewelry.

Beauty, for our purpose, then, is the by-product of interest and pleasure in the choice of action. It is a product of the way each individual makes use of or operates within this framework of interrelationships. If he neglects to consider and is not guided by any one of the forces involved in our diagram, his choice and the results of his work are much less desirable.

From the long struggle of man to produce fine products we can find much help to guide our own efforts. Design, now as in the past, must be concerned with life facts and not just art facts (a point noted by Louis Sullivan). Each era has produced its own interpretation of nature and of life around it. Rarely do we find good designs that are not related to human needs. In fact, there is a valid question whether an object which has no apparent relation to a human need can be legitimately called "good design." Therefore, our approach is to try to provide a laboratory of form, tools, materials, and processes —a place where all you've experienced in the piecemeal fashion of life can become understood and liberated in a medium that lends itself to such an effort.

Before man made his own clothes, he found ways to decorate his body. This indicates a basic psychological urge that still operates in even the most advanced societies. Jewelry is one of the methods man has devised to fulfill this need, and it is as complicated or as naïve as is man himself. By observing jewelry-making in Mexico and the southwestern United States we can understand the development of jewelry over an extensive period of time. Starting with the Chichimecas, the Zapotecas and continuing with the Mayas, the Aztecs, the Mixtecs, and finally with the Navajos, Zuñi, and other Pueblo Indians, we find many examples of fine decorative jewelry. They used many materials—clay, stones, bones, feathers, and finally gold and silver, sometimes in combinations. It was not until recent times (1850–1870) that Navajo silversmiths acquired the skill from the Mexican *plateros* (silversmiths) to produce their own silver ornaments. Each one of these groups developed symbols and forms which are typical of its civilization. Today a little close observation will demonstrate that in spite of our highly developed systems of communication and interrelatedness, jewelry, like the other arts in various parts of the world, developed within a cultural pattern. For example, the silversmiths of northern Europe use much the same materials, processes, and techniques as the *plateros* of Mexico, yet the results are very different. In the United States we find a wide variety in the work of various sections of the country and even more in that of the individual craftsman. In spite of this great variety we also find common characteristics from which our own efforts may be guided.

SOME SOURCES OF IDEAS

* *Nature* All men return to nature for much of their inspiration. We all see pretty much what we look for, but by consciously attempting to look with a realistic, open-minded attitude, we may find new forms and relationships of forms that are definitely our own.

Look around you; check the little things in nature. They will provide many new insights and surprises. Many ideas can be found in scraps of nature. Drift-

Tree forms.

Cactus: the total plant is a mass of forms, and upon closer inspection new and different forms appear.

wood, pebbles, seashells, seedpods, insects—such a list could go on almost indefinitely, and each item has its own individual form. Frank Lloyd Wright, in a lecture to his students, pointed out that the little animals of the sea make better homes for themselves than most human beings do, yet the human is certainly much more intelligent. Do we not have the intelligence to learn from these elementary sources?

* *Surprise box* I have collected bits and pieces of nature for years and keep the collection in an old box. From time to time I return to this source of ideas. It is my "surprise box." Many of my students have found it helpful, and although keeping such a box is just another technique, it can be used successfully by any age group and by the most advanced craftsman. One friend of mine has over the years compiled a collection of sketches, pictures, and real insects until now he has literally thousands from which to obtain ideas. In using such a source of ideas, I am not advocating any copy-cat approach. First, it would be nearly impossible to duplicate many of the things, so why should we try? Second, we are making jewelry, not nature. Finally, our results must include our own reactions and interpretation to be a valid statement. Our problem, as the Buddha pointed out, is to seek and find the cause, and not to copy the effects.

✳ *Try this experiment* Without looking, select some object from a surprise box. Using whatever you pick as a starting point, see what you can do with it. Look at it from all angles. Note any unusual features: shape, texture, line, and their relationships. Make use of the qualities that attract your interest. Chances are they will interest others as well. Decide what you can do to enhance the shape, line, or other effects. Try adding a piece of wire or sheet form. Or combine the two by means of techniques you have already learned. A playful manipulation of each element—points, shapes, and lines: varying them in position, size, and texture—is the shortest way to understanding their relationships.

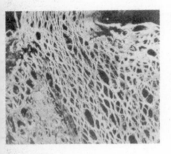

✳ *The arts* Sculpture, painting, graphics, commercial art, and architecture can suggest forms and ideas for your jewelry. Many of these products are the work of the most sensitive and creative people. Often they are far in advance of their own period because they lead, rather than follow, society. As a result, their forms and arrangements of forms are suggestive of a culture. Many books and magazines are available. From this source we have tremendous potential help if we will only use it.

Remember that painting and graphics are two-dimensional and that jewelry is basically a three-dimensional craft. This has one advantage to the craftsman because the forms of necessity can not be

Top: a cactus form. Center: a close-up of weather-worn dead cactus. Notice the fibrous structure that establishes the live cactus form. Close observations of nature will always disclose new shapes and forms. Bottom: a few items from a surprise box.

Top: some sea forms for closer inspection. Center: sculptural forms found on a storm-tossed beach. The shells have been worn away by sand and water. Bottom: some seedpods and a bone found on a field trip.

copied, but must be modified to fit the material. Sculpture and architecture are three-dimensional. In fact, most of the problems of design in these two fields are similar to the design of jewelry. Space, form, tension, organic structure, texture, interpenetration, superimposition, and economy of means—each necessary element plays its role in a unified entity. As you begin to understand that the basic forms (wire–line, sheet–plane, grain–sphere) integrated as a whole constitute design, the lines of demarcation between fine arts, crafts, and industrial design dissolve.

Check some of the many publications that deal with these arts. (See Bibliography, page 169, and some contemporary forms later in this chapter for suggestions.) More important, look at good examples of architecture and visit museums and art galleries.

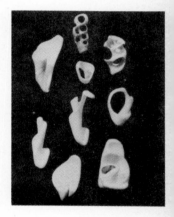

Susanne K. Langer states in her book, *Feeling and Form:* "All making of expressive form is a craft, therefore the normal evolution of art is in close association with practical skills, building, ceramics, weaving and magical practices of which the average civilized person no longer knows the importance; and therefore, also sensitivity to the rightness and necessity of visual or musical forms is apt to be more pronounced and sure in persons of some artistic training than in those who have only a bowing acquaintance with the arts." *

* Susanne K. Langer, *Feeling and Form.* (New York: Charles Scribner's Sons, 1953.)

If jewelry is the creation of forms symbolic of human feeling, it follows that our jewelry will be better as we become more sensitive to the life around us. We can improve this sensitivity in each of us by careful, intelligent observation and application of the life and art in our own environment. As this environment widens, our life becomes more full and enjoyable. The English philosopher Alfred North Whitehead said that "Free activity is often the greatest stretch of which our minds are capable." Is there any better way to expand our lives than to participate in an activity where we can soon control most of the elements involved and relate them to our own and our friends' needs and pleasures? Approached as an experimental craft, the ancient and modern art of jewelry-making is one of the doors to the creative process. And a very pleasant door it is, a thrilling and fascinating activity which is suited to the needs of our time because of its unique and versatile qualities. Because of the freedom which is possible in both technique and design, and because its functional purposes are less restricting than those in the other arts and crafts, jewelry-making has no superior as a medium for motivating and developing original thinking. As jewelry's chief function is to give pleasure, it provides pleasure in the process of creating that pleasure.

Many people of all ages find an answer to the need for manual expression and activity in the manipulation of the materials of jewelry. As you manipulate the materials, you must make decisions and discriminate among various forms, sizes, textures, positions, and the other elements of design, and in so doing find an outlet for your personal esthetic impulses. As a hobby, jewelry-making is neither mentally exhausting nor physically fatiguing and it may be engaged in by people of all ages. Results—as you have already found—are highly satisfying, can be obtained easily and quickly, and give an immediate compensation for the effort expended.

* *Finding your own forms and symbols* We have been discussing sources of ideas for jewelry, not as models to copy, but rather as starting points for your own ideas.

Perhaps, like many others, you have found yourself thinking, "I can not design for myself." You may have convinced yourself that whatever creative ability you once had has completely atrophied. Many people feel this way. The important thing is to find some remedy and to overcome this feeling.

The chances are that you have lost sight of the true impetus which started man making jewelry in the first place. It has become lost in the concern of daily living, or perhaps you are too involved with the techniques as an end in themselves.

Rediscover the urge to manipulate materials and create forms and symbols. Our urge to adorn ourselves, to make symbols for ourselves, is an instinctive one which we all possess, however atrophied it may seem. In many ways it is as natural to want to manipulate materials and make marks and forms as it is to make noises—and for some people more natural.

Remember that jewelry was in its beginning a thing of magic. The hunter painted his body, tied pebbles and bones to his wrists, and stuck feathers in his hair. These were symbols of his power over nature and became part of primitive religious rites. Later, the

decorative devices were refined but were still matters of religion and magic. There is still an element of magic in most of the decorative ornaments we wear. Think how many "lucky charms" and religious pendants are used by modern man.

True, we cannot return to the primitive simplicities or even to a craft-centered society, as advocated during the eighteenth century to cure the ill effects of the Industrial Revolution. Modern life has become much too complex for that. How can we see with the eyes of a child or of primitive men? Why should we try? We *can,* however, encourage some of our latent capacities to emerge from their subconscious depths. As craftsmen, even as beginners, we have already begun to do so. We can learn to see more objectively and to sense more vividly the life and art around us which will bring us closer to better understanding and design. In other less hurried times we can find inspiration.

Here are examples of inventions drawn from the natural life about them, which in essence was not so very much different from our own. Look at the work of artists and craftsmen of the great periods in man's history—from prehistoric and pre-Columbian, through the Hellenic period of Greece to the great medieval religious periods, the Renaissance arts and crafts, and finally take a new look at your own world.

To suggest how man has taken the raw material around him and extracted vital forms and symbols from such simple material, here are a few drawings

Bird and fish forms ranging in time from pre-Columbian to contemporary. Also note the difference between a representation of real lightning and its design form.

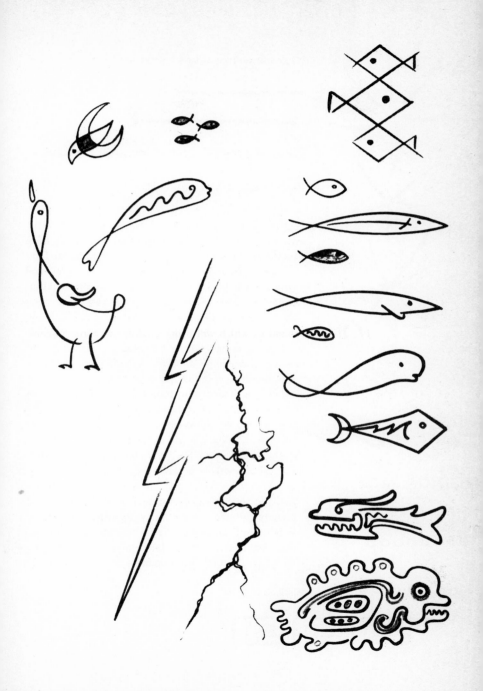

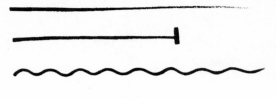

Line in motion and Central point.

selected from many sources. Notice how each artist or craftsman disentangles the essential forms by using the subject in his own way to create an individual expression. Now compare these inventive forms and symbols with dull, commonplace, commercial representations and with photographs. You have seen photographs of lightning. Do they suggest the force, strength, and speed as well as the primitive symbol?

Jewelry design can be a projection of feeling into some visible shape or form. A highly complex or a very simple decoration has what geometric form, for instance, a theorem illustration in geometry does not have—motion and rest, rhythmic unity and wholeness, a kind of kinesthetic energy. A design has, or rather it is, a living form, although it does not represent anything alive. The lines and space of a decoration express vitality in what they themselves seem to do. When they symbolize an animal that might actually do something, that animal is just as likely, and in many cultures is more likely, to be at rest, but the design itself expresses life. The optical or plastic units, organized into spatial configurations, become more than the total of their parts.

Similar elements.

A line in motion tends to remain in motion unless interfered with by some outside force. Lines that intersect a central point radiate from that center, although they never actually change their relation to it. Similar elements repeat each other and create rhythm, unity, and a tendency to be seen together. Dominance can be obtained by position, size, shape, texture, and by all combinations and variations. Note also how variety is introduced in the accompanying illustrations. When considering them together, the "similarity groups" seem to be more unified than "proximity groups."

Textures and colors balance each other. Our list of illustrations could be extended. All these terms and illustrations denote relationships that belong to the object, the created design, and they are just as applicable to the simplest design of a canoe paddle or a piece of jewelry, if the design is artistically sound, as to an easel picture or a piece of sculpture.

Why repeat the trite, the clichés? Why not seek your own forms of symbols from your own ken? Renew your interest and refresh your vision with materials or with pencil, whichever is easier for you. I find both techniques useful myself, and use both interchangeably.

Every time you design and make a piece of jewelry you will be faced with the problem of selecting materials—wire (line), sheet metals (surface), shot, or balls (sphere)—and you're lucky if you can find

Dominance, Size, Position, Texture, and Shape.

or invent new ways every time. It may help you to find
your own forms if you keep in mind some of the basic
concepts of design. One of the most valuable of these
is that of repetition. Repetition is in evidence every-
where as a human expression, from the repeated dot
or line on textiles to the borders of concentric circles
on a formal dinner plate. The symmetrical repeat so
often used by primitive man—the dot, dot, dash,
dot, dot, dash (· · – · · –)—like the beating of a
Mexican concha drum, is an elementary form easily
made visual.

How can we neglect the more complicated forms
of repetition, the variety of nonsymmetrical or in-
formal balance, with its more sophisticated expression
calling forth our sense of balance and selection to a
higher degree? The involved rhythms of nature are
illustrations of relative proportions and sequence.
Contrast, harmony, unity, and movement combine to
control our use of materials, reflective surfaces, trans-
parencies, positive and negative relationships, and
space articulation and structures. All of these, which
provide for us pleasurable visual and tactile reactions or disturb us by their absence, are necessarily
part of the means of design.

SOME DESIGN TECHNIQUES

* *Sketchbook*

You will need a sketchbook or transparent paper,
several good soft pencils, and perhaps a pen for this
type of designing. I prefer a sketchbook of transparent, often called tracing paper, because it can be
laid over previous ideas; changes can then be made
easily. There is another advantage to the sketchbook:

A tracing paper pad makes designing much easier and saves time.

it provides a place to keep your ideas together. I find, however, that after a short time it is desirable to remove the pages from the sketchbook and to keep them in a folder of some sort. At any rate they should be saved for future reference. A soft pencil is better because it offers less resistance and makes a good, definite line. Approach your sketches in a spirit of doodling or scribbling; you are not making pretty pictures but trying to get ideas. Work freely; let the pencil or pen almost guide itself but keep in mind the materials with which you are working or planning to work. When you get something that pleases you, you are ready to control the process. At this point you may place another piece of paper on top of your doodle and trace the design, or perhaps only a portion that you like. In this way change and modify your ideas until you have a plan that really pleases you. Don't wait for ideas; get something down on paper. Inspirations do not arrive in full bloom to inactive minds and bodies. One idea will lead to another.

Design is arrangement, and decoration connotes fitness and formalization. What is fitted is formalized. Even the most elementary design serves to concentrate and hold one's vision to the expanse on which it appears. I have seen painters actually afraid of a new canvas until they could get something on it to destroy its whiteness and sterility. Our problem is to get something in front of us that we can look at and think about. Every time an idea, a line, a form, or

an object is moved, you change its relation to the
other elements and thus produce a new design. This
is not a new experience; we do it all the time in our
daily lives. Only our purpose here is different. We
usually do it, however, with actual objects. Books,
pictures, lamps, flowers, and even our clothes provide us with the experience of arranging elements into
(we hope) desirable arrangements or designs. Man
does have at least one advantage over the lower animals in his ability to imagine, to try out ideas, to pro-
ject those ideas, and to experiment until he finds a
best solution to his problem. All normal people have
this ability, but how well we can visualize an idea is
determined to some degree by past experience. The
beginning craftsman may lack experience; neverthe-
less, as you work with the processes and materials,
you will gain confidence in your imagination. A little
boy, asked how he had made such a nice picture,
replied, "I only thought a thought and just drew
around the think." This experimental approach is
used by most of the good craftsmen I know. If they
have any special ability, it is only that of being more
persistent and patient in their efforts. The beginner
is often much too impatient exactly when he needs
perseverance most.

Once you have something—lines, shapes, and
forms—on paper where they can be moved around,
appraised, and modified, designing can begin in ear-
nest. Now you can make value judgments and evalu-
ate your ideas if you have not already done so. It is
better to have more than one idea to choose from,
and each idea should have a number of variations.
This provides an opportunity to make comparisons
and to exercise your critical judgment.

In addition to the form problems we have been discussing, consideration must at all times be given to other practical implications. Is the piece too large or too small? Is the general form right for the person who will wear it? Perhaps more important, does it *fit* the materials, tools, and processes, and is it within your own skill and experience level in the use of these techniques? If its main function is to create pleasure and interest when worn, you will want to be sure it does achieve that end.

✳ *Models*

Working in a material that approximates the finished object is for many the most effective approach to design. Any pencil-and-paper technique has many limitations, especially for the less experienced craftsman. Perhaps the greatest fault of such techniques is the lack of the third dimension. Models are an important part of our planning in all phases of living. They give us an undistorted concept of form, shape, parts, size, etc., in a more direct and exact means of communicating and developing ideas. Lines on a paper, like words, are inadequate. Models are also a traditional means of communication. Let us then make use of these more exact methods in our jewelry design.

Many materials may be used for the construction of working models. Some that I have used or seen used are: soft metal foil and wire such as lead solder

Top: tinfoil from a cigarette package can provide a designing medium. Opposite: some models made from copper foil (36 gauge). Pliers, shears, and fingers were the only tools used.

or lead sheet, tinfoil, copper foil, and aluminum foil. Baling wire and iron binding wire can serve our purpose. Other materials, such as cardboard, paper, wax candles, soap, clay, and string can be used—anything that is soft and pliable, that can readily be formed with the fingers. Scissors and pliers can be used to produce models. The more nearly these materials duplicate the stretching and forming qualities of the metal to be used in the final construction, the better they serve our aims.

As we work with these materials, many new possibilities will be discovered. To get started, here are some ideas which may aid you. Soft metals in wire or sheet form may be shaped easily with the fingers, and the sheets can be cut with common scissors. Sharper bends may be made with pliers or hammered into various shapes (see Chapter 6). If the metal is placed over a rounded or square form of wood or steel and pounded, it will tend to take the shape of the form. Often only the fingers are needed to rub the metal into the desired form. If a concave shape is used, many more interesting forms may be obtained. The metal may be stretched simply by pounding it with a hammer or a mallet. A steel hammer does the job faster, but it leaves marks on the metal, so decide what effect you want. Don't forget that a hammer also creates an interesting texture upon metals. Many machine-made articles (I am not advocating this), made by lathe or casting, are pounded to give the appearance of hand-hammered metal. This finish is called by the name of the hammer (ball peen) used to create it—a peened metal finish. By contrasting a smooth (mirror or matte) finish with a rough (peened) finish, many interesting combina-

A few items found in a scrap box. Notice the interesting shapes left after a design has been cut out of sheet copper.

tions may be created; this applies to wire as well as sheet metal. Other hammers will give other textures if the metal to be worked is placed upon a smooth steel surface. In this case only the top surface of the metal is affected, but if the metal is placed upon a soft surface—wood, sandbag, or lead block—the marks show in raised form on the opposite side. When wire is used in what often starts out to be an experiment in design, it can actually be turned into a piece of jewelry simply by making a pinback of the two ends or hanging it onto a neckpiece. This is especially true when brass or copper wire or sheet is used, for when any of these has been polished we may have a handsome piece of jewelry.

✷ *Scrap box* (Idea box) The scrap box serves the same purpose as the surprise box and is sometimes more functional, partly because you have made the contents. Many craftsmen maintain such a source of ideas. These bits and pieces of metal and other odds and ends can serve your purpose admirably. The negative shapes left after a form is cut out often provide the basis for future designs when they are bent or shaped and combined with other bits of wire and metal.

Save all your scraps, both from the three-dimensional doodles and models and from the actual materials of the finished jewelry. If you like a neater arrangement, two boxes may solve your problem, one box for the models and one for scraps. But keep them and use them both for future ideas and pieces of jewelry.

DESIGNING IN JEWELRY MATERIALS DIRECTLY

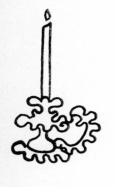

Silver is expensive, but may not be as valuable as your time. Brass and copper are relatively cheap, so why not use them directly? As models are better than other methods, so too is working directly superior to using models. It has most of the advantages of models over other methods and the added advantage of spontaneity. By working directly in the metal many fresh and vitalized designs are produced, often in a relatively short time. Scraps of silver and gold may be sent to the refinery for reimbursement, so if you produce a really unredeemable piece, there is actually little financial loss. Still more important, these scraps can serve a better purpose in stimulating other ideas and designs. A craftsman soon accumulates a supply of wire ends, domes, balls, and odd pieces of sheet metal. These often can be retrieved by melting into shot and discs or fused together to create free forms. If the first experiment does not work, the materials may be used again and again. Most of the jewelers and silversmiths of Mexico and the southwestern Indians of the U.S. produce all their own wire and sheet forms from silver ingots. They have very few and very primitive tools, yet they save every scrap and filing, remelt it and use it to produce some very fine jewelry.

The processes of forming, shaping, cutting, and soldering may be experienced by using a few cents' worth of copper or brass in either wire or sheet form.

If you feel that silver is too expensive, perhaps you will work more freely in these, since you can afford to discard any unpleasing results. After a few forms have been made, they can be combined to create interesting jewelry.

Combinations of various metals—brass on copper, copper on brass, and silver on copper or brass—can produce interesting results. Keep your scraps and odds and ends in the scrap box for future use. Try polishing some of them. See the difference: they may be good enough for use as jewelry.

To summarize—all things have form; most forms are an expression of purpose and have meaning. Any object can be given a great variety of shapes and forms, as illustrated on these pages. Some are appropriate; some are much less desirable.

Masses, textures, and details are treated in terms of the jewelry with an over-all effect in mind, one that is at once personally appealing, structurally and functionally. When a design is architectonic and intellectual, it produces a precise, classic, restrained effect. Free organic forms express fantasy and a rich feeling. Witty and provocative forms can be produced by hammering and fusing. Sculptural, light open forms suggest an emotive response. Useful value and cultural implications also determine the form or the style of an object.

SIGNS OF THE TIMES

The cultural implications of our own modern period, reflected in the painting, sculpture, architecture, and products of industry and technology, cannot be ignored. Some of the forms and symbols of our own cultural pattern are illustrated. Your reaction to these signs and devices may be one of disapproval: "This modern stuff, so what?" or approval: "Now we have something!"—but it is difficult not to react because they are expressive of life about us. Maybe you have never seen an original painting by Cézanne, Picasso, or Mondrian; a sculpture by Archipenko, Henry Moore, or Calder; a house by Frank Lloyd Wright or Le Corbusier; and maybe you have never flown an aircraft, but you will recognize their influence on your daily living. A magazine article a few years ago entitled "You Buy Their Dreams" discussed the influence of the industrial designers on the American consumer. Who and what influence the designer? For an obvious illustration, compare the new architecture with Mondrian's paintings from the 1930s. Other relationships may not be so obvious at first glance, but a little study will soon disclose their original sources.

Today the craftsman expresses himself symbolically, as did the artists and craftsmen of the past. These symbols are in accord with the trends of the time to simplify and to pare down to essentials. Our concern with the space–time dimension, with positive (full) and negative (empty) forms, and with interchangeability is expressed graphically in the signs of the twentieth century. Most of them are now history-painted, carved, constructed, and written about in many books. Science and technology have contributed to these forms. Out of all the art forms you will find that contemporary products generally tend more toward the direct and sensuous than toward the literary. A natural or organic solution is sought for, rather than a rehashing of the timeworn or preconceived concepts. Several fine books to help you get

the feel of this new approach are listed in the Bibliography (page 169).

Possibly there *is* a formula for designing something well, but man has yet to find it. This would imply that products made on the basis of such a formula could not fall short of perfection. The truth is that, in spite of the best use of these elements, there are still many imponderables that cannot be easily defined. After a design is executed, we can rationalize these imponderables and trace them back to facts which are the subject of conscious argument. Our real difficulty arises before the jewelry is made. Practice proves that there is always the possibility of other good solutions with more or less objective qualities.

Let the metal, stones, and tools talk back to you. Listen and feel what they have to say. Don't always impose your will upon them. They can help you if you will only be receptive to their influence, their strength, and their limitations. Combine your impulses and your reason with your knowledge of technique and materials. One without the other is insufficient. When undisciplined impulse is stronger, you have a weak design; when reason is predominant, the design is mechanical and often dreary. We need balance. Liberate yourself, and your jewelry will reflect that freedom.

Reminders

1. Look around you—collect nature for your "surprise box"
2. Save your sketches—"idea folder"
3. Save your scraps—"idea box"
4. Have fun and make jewelry!

10 * COMBINATIONS OF MATERIALS

* *

We are now concerned with extending the range and complexity of our jewelry. This does not mean that the designs will of necessity be more complex, because often the most successful jewelry is the simplest. Jewelry's first function is to enhance the wearer, not detract or divide interest.

The materials treated in this chapter are ones I have used or seen used to create successful jewelry. As these materials and their working characteristics are discussed, we will also consider the problems of joining them to other materials, including metal. Finally, some examples of their use by craftsmen and students will illustrate the application of both materials and techniques. These illustrations should provide you many ideas. If you have followed through the experiments suggested in the chapters on basic technique, you already know most of the techniques you will need for this type of work. If you need to review, check the earlier chapters and Appendix A, page 159.

COMMONLY ACCEPTED EXOTIC HARDWOODS

The revival of interest in wood for jewelry can be accounted for by the almost limitless possibilities hidden in bits and pieces of wood from which beautiful effects can be obtained. As more and more craftsmen, both beginners and those with experience, turn their attention to these materials which offer fresh delights and challenges, many find they must feel their way along in learning how to use woods.

Among the many varieties of wood, the *ebonies* which grow in South America, Ceylon, and the Dutch East Indies are very popular. These come in various shades of dark red and purple-blacks. *Lignum vitae,* the hardest wood known, velvet black in tone, grows in the West Indies and in South America. *Cocabola* from Central America is reddish in color with subtle and varied grain patterns. Some of the *rosewoods* found in Honduras, Brazil, and the East Indies have a fine striped grain in various shades of reddish browns.

The fact that you are not near a good supply of such woods need not be a matter of great concern, for you can obtain them from most jewelry supply houses. Or, perhaps you can find an old piano. The black keys are made of ebony and the cabinets of many old pianos are also made of these woods. Incidentally, this is also a source of ivory, which will be discussed later.

All the exotic hardwoods have desirable properties (color, fine grain, and hardness) that lend themselves to jewelry-making. They can be worked with your jewelry tools, so you need buy no special tools. They can be cut with a jeweler's saw and drilled with hand or electric drills. You can file and polish them much as you do metal. The only finishing material needed is some wax or shoe polish. These woods may be buffed like metal, so there is only one new technique needed.

The one factor that makes working with wood different is the lack of its ability to withstand heat. Wood will obviously burn at the temperatures required to solder metal, so all soldering must be done before the wood is attached. This sometimes poses problems if you do not consider the order in which the various forms must be organized and joined. Since we cannot solder wood to metal, other means must be used. The most commonly used methods are gluing and riveting.

GLUING OR CEMENTING

In Taxco, Mexico, many jewelers use Duco cement to fasten many of their materials together. There are several glues that provide joints nearly as strong and in some cases stronger than the materials joined together. One such glue is Ferris No-Peg Pearl Cement. It has been used for many years to mount pearls, but its use has been expanded with success in setting metal caps on baroque stones. It provides a very strong bond between any of the materials suggested in this chapter. Its one disadvantage is that it must be mixed as it is used. Glyptol cement is nearly as

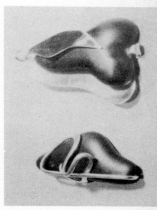

Top: sculptural pendant made from an ebony piano key.
Opposite: Ebony-and-silver pins.

strong as solder and can be used for most materials, including wood, stone, metal, ivory, and bone. Another strong adhesive which can also be used to glue stones together is Opticon No. 220 Epoxy Adhesive and Pit Filler. This glue also needs to be mixed as used. The plastic metal glues, which are really metal in putty form, have good adhesive qualities. They are similar to the body putty used by auto body repair shops; this is ample evidence of their durability and strength.

New adhesives are appearing on the market with such rapidity that you need only check your hardware dealer; if he cannot supply your needs, the supply houses listed in Appendix C can provide the glues suggested.

PRONGS AND RIVETS

An old-standby method of joining wood to metal is by means of prongs wedged, glued, or bent over at the end to form rivets. A hole may be drilled partially through the wood, and a wire the same size as the drill forced into the hole. A drop of glue will add strength to the joint. By drilling the hole completely through the wood and placing into it a wire slightly longer than the thickness of the wood, a rivet can also be formed. Flatten the metal by pounding to make a pressure fit. The excess silver can then be filed flat with the wood to create a decorative accent as illustrated. Additional interest may be added by

Top and center: ebony pendants with inlaid sterling silver. Bottom: ebony and silver cufflinks.

*Opposite: walnut-and-copper fish pin.
Below: polished driftwood-and-silver
pendant.*

varying the size of the holes and the silver. Remember, however, that if a pin is to be soldered to the back or there is to be a backplate the rivets must be soldered before the final fastening to the wood. Small screws or brads may be used to attach pinbacks to wooden pieces.

Metal designs may be laid into the wood to create beautiful contrasts of color and texture. Wood and metal laminates may be made by gluing alternate strips of metal and wood together. Clamp the pieces together with C clamps until the glue is set. This may require several days, but do not rush it. After the glue has set, these built-up pieces may be sawed, drilled, and filed to shape.

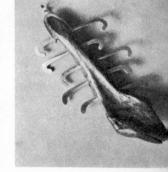

OTHER WOODS

Mahogany and walnut and such fruit woods as apple, cherry, plum, and pear are readily available and provide pleasing contrasts and color when combined with metal. An old tree's interesting knots give form which may be used "as is" since they have such exciting grain swirls and shapes.

Driftwood of all kinds possesses good color and grain; jewelry made from them will reflect the natural beauty. You do not have to live near the ocean to find such materials. Most streams, lakes, and swamps will provide far more usable wood than a craftsman could employ in a lifetime. Generally speaking, although there are exceptions, the hardwoods provide the best pieces for our purpose.

In the southwestern United States and in Mexico I found mesquite to possess beautiful color and grain patterns which combined well with the metals in common use for jewelry. The dried skeletons of cactus have a lacy quality of great interest. Soft desert woods that have been worn away by sand provide interesting forms and shapes.

IVORY, BONE, HORN, AND PLASTIC

The most desirable material in this group is ivory. Many civilizations have recognized its beauty either alone or combined with other materials. The "Snake Goddess" made on the island of Crete about 1500 B.C. is a splendid example. She is about 8 inches high, carved in the round, and decorated with gold. Other ancient and modern societies have also used ivory. The Eskimos and Indians of the American northwest have produced outstanding examples of ivory carvings. Their source of ivory was and is the teeth or tusks of the walrus and other animals. Africa and the Far East have always provided a source of supply and beautiful examples of ivory work. Many supply houses maintain a supply of ivory for the craftsman, if you are interested. Ivory works much like the

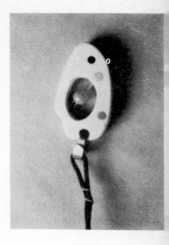

Polished bone-and-copper pendant. A coral bead is suspended in the center.

hardwoods and can be carved, cut, and polished with metal or woodcarving files and tools.

Did you ever consider your roast of beef a source of jewelry material? The meat of course helps provide the energy to work; the waste bones may be used successfully in jewelry. Sometimes during cooking the bones change color and become a muddy brown. These should be bleached either with a household bleach or by allowing the sun and rain to do the job if you have the time. I have found an easier source of bones suitable for jewelry to be the local butcher shop, however. The butcher will probably give you some of Fido's bones; these are usually pretty well empty of meat. This makes your job of cleaning easier. Take a few of the leg bones, cut them in half with a hacksaw, and boil them in salt and soda. Boil the bones for an hour or more until they are clean; remove any scraps of meat or foreign matter, including the marrow. If they still aren't white, soak in bleach water. Remove and put them aside for a few days to dry out; if in a hurry, the oven will do the job faster. Bones prepared in this way have a white ivorylike quality and can be sawed, filed, and worked like wood or ivory. For sawing sections of bone a hacksaw is faster, but your jeweler's saw will do the job. If you have a vise, use it to hold the bone while you are sawing. The bone may be dyed with colored inks. Combined with brass and copper, they can produce fine pieces of jewelry.

Cross sections of bone and horns provide an interesting pattern.

Horn, another excellent jewelry material, is harder for most of us to obtain. Some supply houses stock horn, and you may find some other local source such as a hunter or dairy farmer. Horn varies in color from white to black, with many shades and variations of gray between. Polished, horn provides a lustrous translucent material, and the darker areas create a handsome contrast with silver.

The field of plastics offers so many possibilities that it would require an entire book much longer than this one to cover even a few of them adequately. Plastics can be cast, carved, polished, and worked in many ways. They have been used by craftsmen for some years, but because of their inability to resist scratches by common dust (Mohs' scale 7), they are not too satisfactory in jewelry. If you are interested in experimenting, there are several fine books on the market covering the working properties of plastics.

SEASHELLS

It has been estimated that there are over fifty thousand living species of mollusks, they provide what we commonly call seashells. They are used for decorative and ornamental purposes in both civilized and primitive societies. Shells such as the cowry have long been used as money; pearl, a direct descendant of mother-of-pearl, is one of the most valuable of gems. The inner layer of various seashells is used extensively for jewelry because of its iridescent quality. The abalone

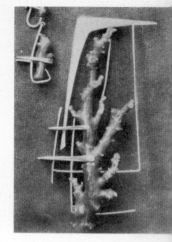

Opposite: a polished coral tree held in a silver construction; prongs to hold the coral. Earrings repeat the Oriental influence. Below: white coral with silver backing and turquoise bead.

is a fine source of beautiful multicolored mother-of-pearl that can be cut with a jeweler's saw and filed into intricate shapes. These shapes can be inlaid into metal to produce distinctive jewelry. For earlier examples of this work look in your grandmother's jewelry box; for contemporary specimens check shops that sell modern Mexican jewelry.

Other shells offer many exciting varieties of shapes, colors, and textures that can provide inspiration, and it is fun to look for them. If you have ever been to a beach, you probably have some shells tucked away someplace around the house. Dig them out and use them as a start for some real pleasure. Personally, I think shells that have been broken and worn away by the tide and sand are the most sculptural and yield opportunity for more improvisation. No new techniques are needed. Use what you already know in a new material combined with metal.

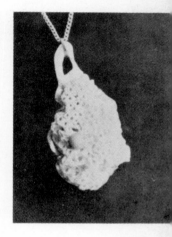

BEACH PEBBLES

Many pebbles of interesting shapes and colors are found throughout the world. These, like the shells, may be turned into conversation pieces of jewelry. They may have little intrinsic value, but as pleasant reminders of happy times they are priceless to you. Wrap, trap, or cage them with a wire that enhances their natural beauty. If you would like to preserve the luster that made you choose the pebble when it was wet, try some of the spray lacquer you used to protect the finish on copper. Lay the pebble on a sheet of paper and spray. Let it dry, then turn it over and spray the other side. Use a thin coat of lacquer. Two thin coats are better than a single thick one. The lacquer will bring out the color and is almost as good as polishing. If you want to do the job right, the stones should be polished by tumbling. Consult any good lapidary book for details of this process.

IDOLS, RELICS, AND OLD COINS

Many primitive civilizations have produced talismans, amulets, charms, and idols which were cut or carved under certain superstitious observances of the heavens or nature to provide good luck and protection from evil. In this category I include ancient coins, bells, and other paraphernalia used by our ancestors. Due to their fragile nature, they are often broken, and we find only pieces, but these may be mounted with metal to protect them from wear and breakage. They can make very charming brooches

Top: large pendant; silver background provides for easy removal of pre-Columbian idol. Opposite: unit jewelry incorporating pre-Columbian artifacts.

and pendants which create interest and appreciation when worn.

This section should call your attention to the possibilities of many materials and objects around you that may be used to create jewelry that will have real meaning to you. By now I hope you have thought of other materials or odds and ends you have collected and put away. A student recently made an attention-getter pin from a small, unidentified animal skull she found. Sam Krammer, a New York jeweler, has used glass eyes in intriguing jewelry. Perhaps you have Grandmother's button box, an old coin collection, or some fascinating seedpods. Get them out and inspect them with this new purpose in mind. You'll see many new possibilities.

A few years ago in one of my classes a very fine technician became interested in the rick rack he found in his wife's sewing box. After experimenting with it he developed several unusual earrings and later made the same earrings in sterling. When I saw him recently, he informed me that these earrings have been so popular among his friends that he has made several dozen pairs. He also said no two pairs are alike. This, remember, is from a machinist who has the skills, techniques, and tools to duplicate anything he wishes. His one big criticism of the jewelry craft is that he no longer seems to find time for his old hobby—fishing.

Look for new combinations as well as for materials that are new to you. Try them out; arrange and rearrange to find the best possible results. Check the sections on jewelry findings and stone settings. You will save time by buying the fittings you need.

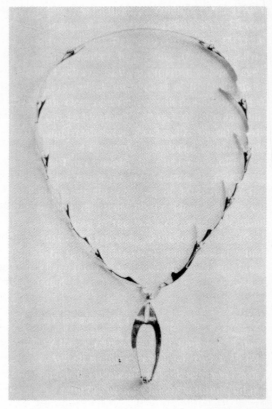

A combination of similar units makes for a striking necklace.

11 * COMBINATIONS OF TECHNIQUES

* * * * * * * * * * * * * * * * * * * *

This is an age of convertibility and interchangeability. Many of our possessions may be used for more than one function and under widely diverse conditions. We have convertible cars, mobile homes; our clothes are reversible and have zipper linings. So why not jewelry that can be worn for different types of social occasions and with various kinds of apparel? It is possible, with a little ingenuity, to use the same piece of jewelry as either a pin or a pendant. Illustrated is a piece of jewelry made several years ago that can be worn in at least a half dozen different ways. By using the neck chain it can be hooked at either end, and both sides are finished so that it is reversible, front to back. Which is front and which is back? I don't know, but either side of the stone, a piece of petrified wood, has pleasing color and texture, and in my opinion is equally handsome. The S-shaped gizmo in the illustration is really a pinning device which clips into the holes at each end of the piece. Here again there are several ways it can be worn as a pin. For added adaptability, another piece of jewelry using a piece of polished sodalite was made

139

which can be hung on the same neckpiece. Any number of jewelry pieces could be hung using only one
necklace.

Many stones, shells, and metal forms look equally
good from several positions, so why not plan your
design to use more than one side of the object? Often
a completely different effect is obtained by simply re-
versing a pendant. This does require better design
ability and craftsmanship to solve the problems of
the holding devices. When you are working with wire
an extra loop may add interest to your design and

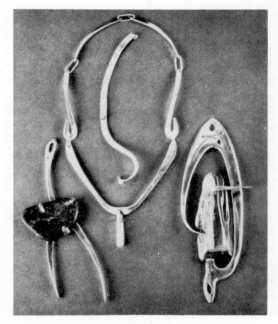

Convertible jewelry, showing various parts.

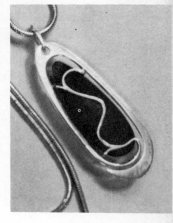

Bloodstone pendant, showing both sides.

also make it possible to hang or pin the jewelry in more than one position.

A cabochon stone may be set so that the back of the setting is just as attractive as the front, as illustrated by the pendant with a bloodstone. The stone is well protected but is set to enhance its beauty from both sides.

To convert a brooch to be used as a pendant requires a loop or hook which can be soldered to the back. Some jewelers provide for this on many of their pieces. Another method makes use of a piece of tubing slightly shorter than the pin tang. The tubing is soldered to a backpiece fitted with a loop and necklace. The pin of the brooch is simply slipped through the tube and fastened.

To reverse the process, a pinning device can easily be devised to provide for wearing a pendant as a brooch. A piece of rectangular wire with a hooking

Using scraps to convert pins to pendants.

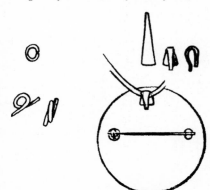

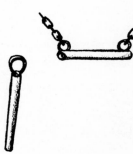

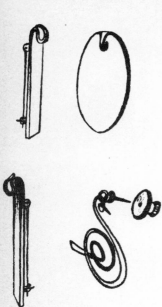

Several methods of converting pendants to pins.

arrangement at the top needs only a pinback for completion. You may think of other possibilities— such as earrings to be worn as scatter pins by using a clutch back or tie-tack findings, and possibly earrings that can be worn as rings.

MOBILE OR UNIT JEWELRY

Moving parts often add additional variety and introduce the feeling of spaciousness so in vogue in our time. The shapes themselves may be abstract and can continue to exist as independent units of the whole. They need the unity of similar shapes, texture, or material. Try to keep the connectors part of the structure or design rather than something added. Jump links work well but sometimes detract from the design and can often be eliminated by a little planning. A few simple methods of flexible joints are shown in the sketches. (See also *Findings,* Chapter 2).

Earrings that dangle add sparkle. Necklaces, bracelets, and brooches may have similar units and when worn together add distinction to most clothing.

A method to extend mobile jewelry further and to increase its flexibility is the provision for detachable

A variety of connecting elements which can be used to attach parts to the basic piece. See also the necklace on page 138.

Top and center: small units of bent, twisted, and spiraled wire were combined to create these earrings. Bottom figures: sterling beads, plain and decorated with wire spirals.

parts. An earring may be changed completely by adding or subtracting a dangle to fit the wearer's mood or occasion. This poses no great technical problem, as hooks or loops similar to the ones discussed earlier may be used.

ADDITIONAL TECHNIQUES

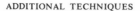

* *Marriage of metals* An interesting technique developed in Taxco, Mexico, by Tony Castillo and others is that of combining various metals into a flat surface. It is used not only for jewelry but also for hollowware. Many subtle and beautiful effects can be obtained, depending upon the variety of colors of the metals used for contrast. Briefly, the process consists of cutting designs of various metals and solder-

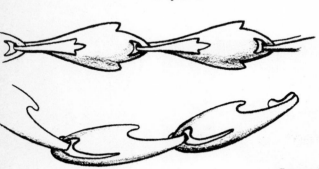

ing them together onto a flat surface. When silver is used with a high-melting silver solder, it is almost impossible to see the joints of the various metals, whence the name of the process.

In experimenting with this process I found an easy procedure. Select a shape and design and make one each of the outside shape in copper, brass, and silver. Place the design on one of the three pieces. Clamp them together for sawing. By sawing all three pieces at the same time, all cuts and pieces are exactly alike so that they are interchangeable. After they are cut out and separated, the pieces may be arranged to develop the best design. To join the several pieces, place them on a flat asbestos or wire soldering base. Be sure the pieces are well fluxed and use plenty of solder. Try to heat the piece evenly by using a fairly large flame. Check all your joints. If more solder is needed to fill any holes, add more flux and solder. Pickle, clean, and polish the piece as directed in Chapter 3.

Connecting units are an integral part of the design rhythm.

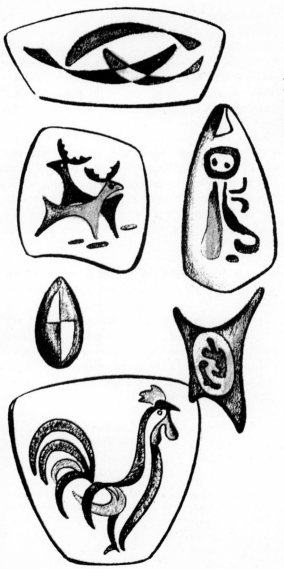

Area designs may be achieved by the "marriage of the metals" technique. Work carefully and compensate for the thickness of the saw blade.

Although this technique lends itself to the creation of area designs, lines may be used. Saw the line out of the background metal with a blade the thickness of the metal you wish to use to make the line. Rectangular wire is good, or thin metal strips about a sixteenth of an inch wide may be cut. Place this metal in the saw cut, solder and file down to the level of the surrounding metal. Dots may be made in a similar manner, by drilling holes and placing wire of contrasting metal into them. After they are soldered, the dots are filed flat to match the metal around them.

The final form may be shaped into concave or convex shapes after all soldering is completed by pounding the piece over a stake or into depressions in a lead block, dapping block, or any other form you have available.

* *Sandwiched decoration*   Feathers, abalone shell, and other thin materials may be sandwiched between two pieces of metal for another technique that adds variety to a craftsman's repertoire. Feathers have played an important part in Mexican culture since early pre-Columbian times. There are many references to feathers in the Aztec codes. These bright feathers have also been used extensively for jewelry. This technique, a recent development, utilizes the color of the feathers by saw piercing a design out of the front piece of metals. The feathers are cut and glued behind the metal. A backpiece of metal with the appropriate jewelry findings attached is then

Interesting color and texture is provided by sandwiching various materials, such as feathers, between cut-out forms.

riveted to the front to provide a durable setting for the feathers. To make the rivets drill holes in the two pieces of metal and solder wire the same size into the front piece before the feathers are arranged. When you put the metals together, place these wires through the corresponding holes in the backpiece and pound to form the rivet. If the jewelry is to have a convex or concave surface, it is best to pound the two shapes over a stake at the same time; this can be done either before or after the design has been cut out of the front piece.

THE COMPLETE PROCESS

By developing an idea taken at random into a piece of jewelry, let us examine the complete working process. I do not mean to imply that this is the only procedure, but rather to suggest a possible approach that has helped students and hobbyists find an integration of ideas, materials, and techniques. The illustrations which follow will amplify your understanding of this integration.

The next example shows some doodles made on a napkin from one of my idea folders. I sketch ideas on envelope backs, napkins, newspaper margins, or almost anything handy. (My students have developed excellent pieces of jewelry from sketches made while listening to lectures, sitting around the snack bar, or telephoning.) My ideas are stored in a folder of design notations (idea folder) and sometimes I get around to putting them into better form in a sketchbook. Even though (as in this example) the design is conceived as a flat linear design, the metal and the tools keep the idea flexible until the end, and the result has

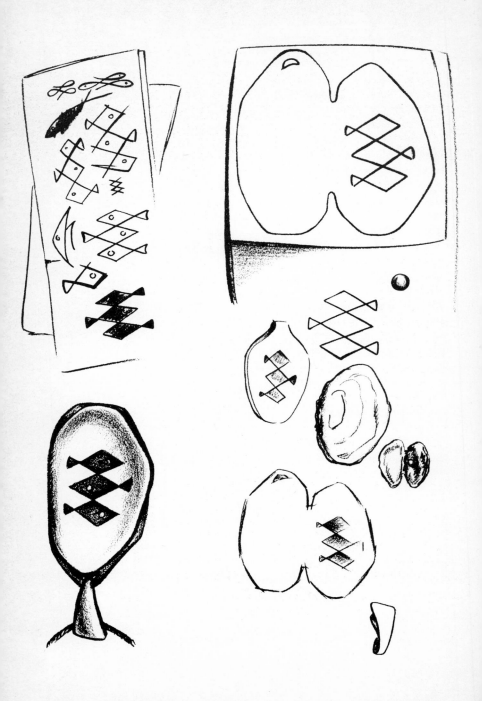

a sculptural, three-dimensional quality suitable for jewelry.

This piece started with a pearl—suggesting water, sea, fish, and seashells. Fish, a symbol of early Christianity, friendship, fertility, and plenty. Fish, pearly-eyed—fish and the Trinity. Threeness? Can it work? Use the pearl as an eye and perhaps some shot or holes to repeat the roundness. Cut out the fish. Silver is best for a pearl setting. Add some wires—make lines; lines can emphasize fish forms. It might work, but too many points. Jewelry shouldn't have too many points—jab into wearer. Not so good. What other possibilities are there? Maybe a shape around the fish? *That's it!* Pearls come from oysters. Why not an oyster shape? Can it work? Certainly it will. Oysters are bivalve mollusks—two parts to shell, a front, a back; just right. Two pieces of silver. No, I can fold the metal—one piece will do nicely. Saw-pierce the front, using the three-fish doodle—makes a nice combination of positive and negative shapes. A hole can have as much shape-meaning as a solid mass. The negative shape is the intended and considered form. Antique the back—make the fish black. Show off pearl's luster to best advantage. But how to mount the pearl in a hole? Put it on a peg soldered to the back—raise it up to make it important.

What final shape should the outside form be? There are thousands of possibilities. Try this one. The fold can go at the top and can also serve as a hanger for the pendant. No. Too weak for this size; wrong shape—oysters open from the side. I'll try it. However, the fold will make a straight edge. That's fine—gives more repetition of the straight lines in the fish. Yes, the side fold is best. It fits. Reverse the front—make it concave, not convex; help protect the pearl. Pearls grow inside oysters—mother-of-pearl layer. Don't let it (the pearl) stick up too high. Pearls are too soft—need protection from scratches and wear. Change the back shape, make it different. This isn't an oyster, it's a pendant. Cut out the shape. How does it look? Too big here—cut more away.

On and on it goes with a continuous searching and modifying of ideas, shapes—selection and elimination of materials and techniques until you are satisfied with the results. Sometimes the sketches may be developed to completion as suggested in Chapter 10, but usually they must be modified as the piece of jewelry develops. By the time a piece is finished, you should know how to make it better, and your next piece of jewelry will always be your best one. As you gain experience, you will be better able to anticipate the effects of the metals, tools, and techniques and plan their improvement.

But let us complete this pendant. Some of the problems are solved, at least partially. Or are they? What gauge silver is best for this size? Twenty gauge is thick enough for strength, especially when it is formed over a stake. But for appearance would eighteen gauge be better? No, it isn't any better and would add to weight and cost. Twenty gauge is right.

Glue the final paper shape to the silver with rubber cement. Arranging it this way will save metal and make it easier to cut. Cut it with the shears to save time. Where's that mallet? Need it to flatten the metal again. File the edges. Drill a hole for the saw blade. Is that blade tight enough? A little wax will reduce the saw's binding. Patience: don't force the saw; keep the lines straight; be careful in the corners—means less filing. The sawing's completed—didn't break a blade! Raise the metal a little before starting the fold. Get the shape right—not too much, just the edges. That's good. OK—now for the fold. Bend it around a nail held in the vise—easier that way and better control. Not bad, but it needs more curve—pound it a little here. Much better, but there is still a lot of filing to be done. The holes for the eyes: mark them with a center punch and drill them. Make the peg. Drill the pearl (better be careful with that drill). This pearl is too good to spoil. Make a start with a scriber. Not too much pressure with that drill— take it easy! Try the wire peg: want a nice snug fit. OK, we can pound the other end to make a better contact with the backpiece, and it will also be easier to hold it in place while soldering. That solder job was easy—now to pickle and clean the piece. It's ready to polish. No—here is a spot that needs more filing, and that edge isn't right yet. Where did that scratch come from? I thought I was being careful. Emery paper will remove it. Now for the steel wool. I am finally ready to polish the piece. The muslin wheel with tripoli compound on it is just the thing for a start. Charge the wheel again. That's cutting better. Needs a little more polishing here to remove that spot. Now for the rouge wheel. Wash the piece first. This is a chore, but it has to be done. Keep changing the position—not too much buffing in one place. That's a good finish—look at it shine! Wash off the grease and rouge (use a tooth brush); get it out of the corners. If there is going to be a good, even coat of oxidized metal, it has to be clean. Is the liver of sulphur strong enough? It must be—getting a nice

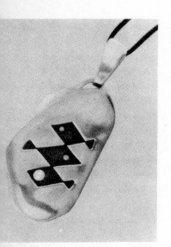

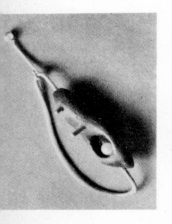

black color. That's enough. Wash it again. Remove the color where it isn't wanted. Don't use steel wool on this (too coarse) but the front can be buffed with the rouge wheel. A buffing stick will do those hard-to-get-at places and the polishing cloth will complete the operation. Fine. How does the pearl look? Nice. That's just right, so let's glue it to its peg and make the neckpiece while the glue is drying.

This pendant, a relatively simple one requiring easy techniques, has been completed in about four hours from start to finish—including the hanging device made from a few scraps of sheet silver. The necklace is simply a piece of black nylon cord with a silver catch. After the first pendant, additional ones have been made, three or four at a time. I can turn out four of them in about six hours by working all four simultaneously. They are cut out with a jeweler's saw, filed, drilled, and saw-pierced at once by using a clamp to hold the pieces together. They are all formed over the mandrel, soldered, polished, antiqued, and buffed at the same time.

As you can see, a great deal of time is saved by making several pieces at once. In fact, many students have found that by having more than one piece of jewelry in process at the same time they accomplish more even though the pieces are quite different in character. One idea usually leads to another, so keep working.

Another piece of jewelry using a pearl was developed over a period of several weeks by a student. The driftwood was found on the beach and used as found except to polish it with neutral shoe polish to add luster to the gray color and bring out the black of the hole.

Sheet-metal forms were discarded in favor of the wire shape which repeated the wood form and provided a balancing element. The pearl was added at the end and proved to be the just right note to accent and complete the piece.

The crosses on the next page required more complicated planning and techniques. The top cross uses an opal as a focal point. The large cross was forged from quarter-inch square wire, using only hammers and files. Gold provides the accent for the center. The smaller cross to the left makes use of amethysts and small units of wire to provide the surface design. The sketches below illustrate the development of ideas for the first two crosses.

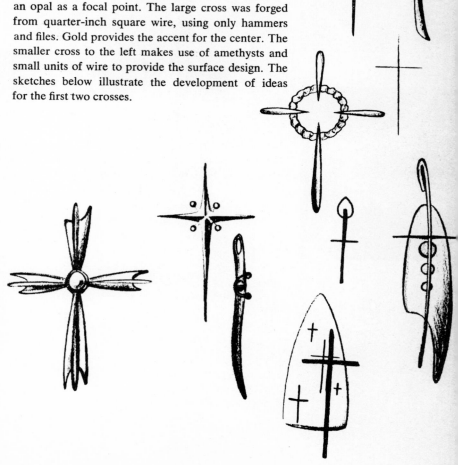

Top: sterling-and-fire-opal cross. Bottom right: sterling-and-gold cross. Bottom left: sterling-and-amethyst cross.

12 *EVALUATION

* *

Jewelry, like other crafts, has a large appeal today. Of those attracted to it, none are more appreciative of its value than those individuals who are engaged in a specialized occupation. In these days of intensive specialization, boundaries of activity are more or less defined, and the time element is often emphasized.

Jewelry-making offers a wide scope for creativity when an individual has acquired a fair degree of skill. Since for many its practice is mainly avocational, the jewelry craftsman is free to work leisurely with imagination and complete independence. He can create, develop, and produce a product alone, as a personal responsibility, and the result represents an individual achievement.

Further satisfaction comes from the fact that the product, aside from whatever distinctiveness it may have, is generally one of utilitarian or decorative value. Jewelers make many pieces for themselves, as gifts for friends and family, and some find a ready market for their work.

155

CRAFTSMEN'S GUILDS

Many communities throughout the country have organized craftsmen guilds. Some have been in existence many years, stimulating the desire for honest craftsmanship and have made it possible for many beginners to learn the craft when few other sources of instruction were available. The mutual exchange of ideas within the guilds has exerted considerable influence on nationwide jewelry trends.

Guild members in some areas have contributed their time and experience to hospitals, assisting therapists in their work with patients. In the field of therapy, jewelry-making has received general recognition as a corrective medium. The therapist's work begins upon the recommendation of the doctor and is used chiefly for rehabilitation, for mental and physical restoration, and for prevocational training for the handicapped. Many metal techniques are easily adapted to the individual needs of the patient in effecting the desired therapy.

THERAPEUTIC VALUE

Successful therapy involves a combination of physical and mental stimulation. Each case must be considered as a separate problem; but with whatever equipment used—hammer, saw, pliers, or other tools and materials—the mental attitude is frequently as important as the physical activity. The patient's interest may be stimulated by bits of wire and sheet metals or perhaps by some colorful stones which should, whenever possible, be selected by the patient. In cases where the therapy has been carried over into the vocational rehabilitation program of the patient, he has in many instances found a ready market for his products.

EDUCATION

Educators, both art teachers and industrial arts teachers, are finding jewelry a promising medium for the realization of their educational objectives at all educational levels. I have had graduate and under-graduate students tell me how much better they were able to understand their pupils and their pupils' prob-lems because of their work in jewelry. Some students have stated that they have learned more from a course in creative jewelry about general education than in many educational courses. Most of these state-ments have been made by students at the end of their first short jewelry course. I believe it is the result of their being exposed to a new medium and in a sense being able to work in a manner very similar to their own students—in short, a new problem-solving situ-ation but on their own adult level. The informality of the experimental method and comradeship which inevitably comes when craftsmen work together in a creative way, plus the natural interest generated by the medium, produce a wholesome social situation in the classroom. When the teacher is considered as one of the group, exploring, experimenting, and en-joying the work along with the class, both students and teacher can learn a great deal from each other. Such a desirable classroom situation is natural and al-most inevitable in a jewelry class where the emphasis is upon individual creative work.

INDIVIDUAL POSSIBILITIES

There is a group of jewelers interested in individual expression. This group seeks adventure in the search for new and interesting combinations of materials and techniques. Such jewelers devote much time to designing and experimenting to arrive at critically correct integrations of form, metal, and stones for a given personality and costume.

The work of these jewelers is found in competitive exhibitions, and some have been chosen for permanent museum and private collections. Though few hand jewelers design expressly for commercial jewelry manufacturers, many of their pieces that show promise of being adapted to mass production are acquired by the industry. On the other hand, manufacturers of jewelry who are looking for the unusual often turn to the hand craftsman as a consultant or designer.

It is difficult to make a transposition of a handmade piece of jewelry to mass production without losing much of its character. Conversely, hand craftsmen soon realize that it is pointless to attempt certain processes that can be best done with precision stamps and machines. Large stamping presses and casting machines as well as the complex finishing equipment used for making commercial jewelry are highly technical devices and, as such, operate with mechanical precision. Hand tools should be considered rather as instruments since the product, being humanly controlled and operated, in many ways reflects the individual temperament of the craftsman. In this respect, every piece of handmade jewelry may be said to bear the personal imprint and signature of its maker.

APPENDIX A: SOLVING YOUR PROBLEMS

Problems	Cause	Solution
Breaks or cracks in metal (wire or sheet)	Metal is too hard, has been worked too much.	Anneal to return the metal to its soft, pliable state. (See Chapter 4)
Rough surface texture on annealed metal	Too much heat.	Use a soft yellow flame all over the metal. Do not heat above recommended temperatures. (See Chapter 4)
Pits in metal after heating	Lead or other foreign materials on the metal that concentrate the heat.	Remove any soft solder or lead (lead block) with steel wool and wash in water before applying heat.
Gray areas on silver	Fire scale, red oxides of copper formed on the metal by excessive and/or prolonged heat.	Remove fire scale from most jewelry by additional polishing. For really persistent spots use emery paper, a scotch stone, or a bright-boy eraser in order to remove the gray and to re-expose clean metal.

or

Heat to dull red. Be careful not to melt solder. Pickle, wash with stiff brush, soap and water. Repeat three times.

or

Dip in a half water, half nitric acid solution (bright dip). Be careful, as only a few seconds are required. A longed dip may eat away too much metal.

No solder joint	Three most common causes are lack of tight fit, dirt, and no flux.	Check for cleanliness. Use your scraper to insure a bright clean surface at the joint. Be sure the two pieces fit snugly and flux both surfaces before binding. (See Chapter 4)
Solder balls up but does not flow	Dirt or heat is applied to solder rather than whole piece.	Grease or oxides will retard the solder from flowing. Flux will help clean the metal, but check for cleanliness. Heat should be applied to the whole piece and not concentrated on the solder until just before it flows.
Solder flows away from joint	Solder flows toward the hottest point.	By carefully controlling the heat, you may pull the solder to the spot you want it. A sharp blue flame is hottest.
Removing oxides	Base metals when hot form oxides.	Pickle is usually sufficient to remove oxides. Reheat the piece and drop into the pickle. This may be done several times without harm to the jewelry.
Removing fire-hardened flux	Flux becomes a glasslike substance when heated beyond its melting point.	Use your file or scraper to get large drops off the metal. Then reheat and pickle.
Solder shows at joint or on metal	Too much solder was used.	Reduce the amount of solder to save work. File or scrape excess solder away. Sometimes it is advisable to remelt the solder, but be sure to use more flux.
Rough granular surface texture or cracks in metal.	Too much heat.	When silver is heated above 1400°, the grain size increases. Additional heat may cause fusion. Use a less-hot flame and do not concentrate it in one place. It produces an interesting surface texture that is highly desirable on some jewelry.

Removing grease and finger marks	Even clean fingers have grease and oil on them. Buffing compounds contain wax or grease.	Wash in a solution of ammonia and baking soda, commercial metal cleaners, or with kitchen cleanser. Water should flow evenly over the surface when the metal is clean. If drops form, it is not clean.
Spotty antiquing or oxidization	Dirt, grease, or oxides.	Clean as suggested above to insure a bright clean metal surface.
Removing antiquing or oxidization	Oxides form on metal exposed over a long period of time.	Antiquing may be removed by buffing, using steel wool or pumice powder. Control the process and remove only the oxidization from the high spots.
Scratches or flaws in inaccessible areas	Poor planning.	Sometimes the metal must be polished before joining. Scrapers, burnishers, and riffle files will work into difficult spots. Often these areas may be oxidized to cover the defects.
Opening and closing jump rings		Always open jump rings sideways, not in the round direction. Then it is a simple operation to reclose them.
Bezel too small	Faulty measurement.	Place bezel over a metal bezel or ring mandrel and tap lightly all around the bezel with a steel hammer. Repeat if necessary until the bezel fits snugly but not too tight.
Bezel too large	Faulty measurement.	Place an auto-point file in a vise, then place the bezel joint on either side of the file and, locking the fingers to assure steadiness, file both sides of the bezel at one time. This insures a good joint. If the bezel has been soldered, use a jeweler's saw to cut the bezel. Often the thickness of the saw blade will remove enough metal to make a fit.

Metal bezel or prongs too hard to force against the stone	Working metal hardens it and makes it springy.	Anneal the metal to reduce the tension. Be careful not to melt the solder joints. After annealing the metal, it should work easily and should not spring back when forced against the stone.
Scratches show up on buffing	Too much of a hurry to finish.	Don't continue to buff or polish. Go back to steel wool or emery cloth. It will save time. Usually continued buffing will make the scratches deeper.
Removing stone from bezel	They often stick when checking for fit.	Put some sealing wax on a stick and warm until it becomes sticky. Stick the wax to the stone and cool. When cool, pull the stone out or run a sharp tool such as a knife around between the stone and bezel to loosen.

TOOLS AND EQUIPMENT

Basic set of hand tools (cost about $15)

Chain-nose pliers with cutter

6″ half-round smooth-cut file (Swiss pattern)

Ball peen hammer

Rawhide mallet, 1½″ face

Set of three needle files: round, half-round, three-square

Hand drill and twist drills (small sizes)

Jeweler's saw frame (adjustable) (4″ throat), jeweler's saw blades size 1

Aviation or Wiss shears

Buffing stick

Burnisher

Bench pin or V board and clamp

These are the basic hand tools for making jewelry—sufficient for sawing or cutting out a shape, giving it dimension and form, bending wire, saw-piercing, filing, and finishing. A wide variety of jewelry can be made using just these tools and the general supplies listed below.

General supplies

Emery cloth (fine)

Steel wool, grades 0 to 000

Jeweler's rouge

Rule (steel or steel edge desirable)

Dividers or compass

Tweezers (pointed)

Handy flux for hard soldering

Paste flux for soft soldering

Small brushes (two or three)

Sulphuric acid for pickle

Glass jars or Pyrex baking dishes for acids

Liver of sulphur

Hardwood blocks

Hardwood dowels (can be used for mandrels, etc.)

Scriber (sharp-pointed metal tool—ice-pick, fingernail file, etc.)

Center punch

Cloths

If you buy them all new, they shouldn't cost more than $10. The addition of soldering equipment listed below will increase your potentialities.

Basic Soldering Equipment

Berns-O-Matic or a similar self-contained Propane gas unit with disposable tank will provide an adequate source of heat and only costs about $5 in hardware stores. New tanks of gas cost about $1.50 and last for fifteen hours.

Mouth blowpipe and rubber hose to connect to your gas outlet or kitchen range is a good basic heat source and is safest for the beginner. It does require learning to blow and breathe practically at the same time, which poses a problem for some people. Cost about $2.50.

A foot bellows and hand torch provide a good source of heat with natural or manufactured gas. Cost about $20.

Asbestos soldering pad, one 12″ × 12″ and one 6″ × 6″ are adequate. Common unglazed fire bricks will work.

Charcoal blocks reflect the heat and make soldering much easier.

Hand tools to be added later
These tools make some jobs much easier and extend the range of your jewelry, especially if you set up your own shop:

Round-nose pliers
Half-round-nose pliers
Ring clamp or hand vise
Bench vise
Hand file
Set of needle and riffle files
Various hammers and stakes (check your catalogue for tool types available)

Soldering pan (annealing pan)
Ring mandrel
Dapping block, punches or dies
Metal gauge
Bench block or anvil
Scraper

Sometimes these can be found in junk or secondhand shops. Don't buy cheap tools. The quality is usually so inferior as to make them almost worthless. You will also find other specialized tools that might interest you, but don't buy them until you feel the need for them.

Some machines that save time and money
Buffing machine. Available from about $25 up, plus buffing wheels. An old electric motor can be used.

Flexible shaft machine. Cost about $35 and up, plus various cutting, grinding, and polishing tools, the variety of which is almost unlimited.

Your dentist will give you his old drills, and they make fine tools. A flexible shaft and adapter that may be attached to most motors is available for $9 to $10. The

small hand grinder may be used, but I find that the torque they produce reduces their usefulness.

A Prest-O-Lite soldering unit makes a good all-purpose source of heat; it costs only about $45 complete.

APPENDIX C

Try local sources first—hardware and department stores, hobby shops, and your local jewelers.

There are many fine dealers throughout the country; wherever possible choose one near at hand. I list only a few sources that I have personally found to be very cooperative. In general my students have also found them helpful in supplying information and catalogues as well as fast and courteous service. This list in no way implies that other dealers are not reputable.

General tools and equipment
These sources stock most of the items needed by the jewelry craftsman and have good to excellent catalogues.

Allcraft Tool and Supply Co., Inc.
15 West 45th Street
New York 36, N.Y.

Anchor Tool and Supply Co.
12 John Street
New York 38, N.Y.

William Dixon, Inc.
32 E. Kinney Street
Newark 1, N.J.

Southwest Smelting and Refining Co.
1710 Jackson Street
Dallas 21, Texas

Grieger's Inc.
1633 E. Walnut Street
Pasadena 4, Calif.

C. R. Hill Co.
35 W. Grand River
Detroit 26, Mich.

The metals (in addition to the above)
T. B. Hagstoz and Co.
709 Samson Street
Philadelphia 6, Pa.

Hoover and Strong, Inc.
111 W. Tupper Street
Buffalo 1, N.Y.

Semi-precious and precious stones (check Lapidary Journal)
John J. Barry Co.
Book Building
Detroit, Mich.

Sam Kramer
W. 8th Street
New York 11, N.Y.

Semi-precious and precious stones (cont'd.)
Ernest W. Beissinger
415 Clark Building
Pittsburgh 22, Pa.

Ward's Natural Science Establishment, Inc.
P.O. Box 1712
Rochester 3, N.Y.

International Gem Co.
15 Maiden Lane
New York 7, N.Y.

BIBLIOGRAPHY

PHILOSOPHY

Rudolf Arkeim, *Art and Visual Perception,* University of California Press, Berkeley, 1954

John Dewey, *Art as Experience,* Minton, Balck and Co., New York, 1934

Susanne K. Langer, *Feeling and Form,* Charles Scribner's Sons, New York, 1953

Edward Mundt, *Art, Form and Civilization,* University of California Press, Berkeley, 1952

Brewster Ghiselin, *The Creative Process,* University of California Press, Berkeley, 1952

DESIGN AND DRAWING

Calvin Albert and Dorothy G. Seckler, *Figure Drawing Comes to Life,* Reinhold, New York, 1957

Yvonne Françoise Jossic, *1050 Jewelry Designs,* Albert A. Lampl, Philadelphia, 1946

Gyorgy Kepes, *Language of Vision,* Paul Theobald, Chicago, 1944

L. Moholy-Nagy, *Vision in Motion,* Paul Theobald, Chicago, 1947

Simon Nicalaides, *Natural Way to Draw,* Houghton Mifflin, Boston, 1941

Paul Rand, *Thoughts on Design,* Wittenborn, Schultz, New York, 1951

Henry M. Rasmusen, *Art Structure,* McGraw-Hill Book Company, Inc., New York, 1950

MATERIALS AND TECHNIQUES

John Adair, *The Navajo and Pueblo Silversmiths,* University of Oklahoma Press, Norman, 1945

William T. Baxter, *Jewelry, Gem Cutting and Metal Craft,* McGraw-Hill Book Company, Inc., New York, 1950

Murray Bovin, *Jewelry Making,* published by author, New York, 1959

Margaret Craver, *Making Hand Wrought Sterling Silver Jewelry,* Handy & Harman, New York, 1945

Emil F. Kronquist, *Metalcraft and Jewelry,* Manual Arts Press, Peoria, 1926

Leslie L. Linick, *Jewelers Workshop Practices,* Henry Paulson Co., Chicago, 1948

Greta Pack, *Jewelry and Enameling,* D. Van Nostrand Co., New York, 1953

Charles J. Martin, *How To Make Modern Jewelry,* Museum of Modern Art, New York, 1949

MATERIALS AND TECHNIQUES (cont'd.)

Andrew Dragunas, *Creating Jewelry for Fun and Profit*, Harper & Brothers, New York, 1947

W. Ben Hunt, *Indian Silversmithing*, Bruce Publishing Co., Milwaukee, 1952

Emil F. Kronquist, *Art Metal Work*, McGraw-Hill Book Company, Inc., New York, 1942

Arthur and Lucille Sanger, *Cabochon Jewelry Making*, Charles A. Bennett Co., Peoria, 1951

Lewis Wiener, *Hand Made Jewelry*, D. Van Nostrand Co., New York, 1948

D. Kenneth Winebrenner, *Jewelry Making*, International Textbook Co., Scranton, 1953

PAMPHLETS AND CATALOGUES—a very good source of information

"Craft Metals," T. B. Hagstoz & Co., Philadelphia (price 75 cents)

"Encyclopaedia and Super-Catalogue of Lapidary and Jewelry Arts," Grieger's Inc., Pasadena, 1957 (price $3.95)

"Silver for the Craftsman," Handy & Harman, New York, 1946

"Design Quarterly," No. 45–46, 1959, Walker Art Center, Minneapolis, Minn. (price $1.50)

MAGAZINES

Crafts Horizon, American Craftsman's Council, New York

Lapidary Journal, Del Mar, California
Gems and Minerals, Mentone, California